THE MENDING HEART

Harvest House Publishers
Irvine, California 92714

Dedicated to
God, the Master Mender
and to
My Family

The Scripture quotations in this publication are from the **Revised Standard Version Bible,** copyright 1946, 1952, ©1971, and 1973 by the Division of Christian Education, National Council of the Churches of Christ in the U.S.A., and are used by permission.

THE MENDING HEART

Copyright ©1979 by Harvest House Publishers
Irvine, California 92714

Library of Congress Catalog Number 79-84746
ISBN 0-89081-201-2

All rights reserved. No portion of this book may be reproduced in any form without the written permission of the Publisher.

Printed in the United States of America.

Preface

It would not be right to send out this book on recovery of wholeness without a few words of acknowledgment. First, I must express gratitude to William Barclay, Langdon Gilkey and Ernest Gordon, each the author of insightful analyses of revelations made to persons caught in despair. Relatively few people are gifted enough to sketch clearly the inner torment experienced by countless human beings struggling against self and life's conditions. The Christian faith for me has been sharply lifted by these writers with a most convincing warmth and simplicity, lifted to where I have been better able to address the key issues involved in coping with despondency. My sense of debt to them continues as a treasured reminder of the beauty of the Word.

The theme of this book is the inner reunification achieved by God through Christ. A second acknowledgment must be made of my thanks for all those who have brought the Word to me—my family, the church, Christian writers and others who have come to me in their varied dilemmas. Allowing God to bind our hurts is an incredibly simple, liberating process; yet one that becomes lost or distorted. Closing off God so often seals us from the mending we seek and for which we ache. Laden beneath disappointments and plagued with old habits, we desperately require a new strategy for coping. The elusive health we crave at times (or the plain relief we cry for) requires some reordering of perspectives, often under circumstances far less than ideal. The mission outreach, however, comes directly from God, together with His mercy, and also through others who embody and carry the gospel. I am deeply grateful to God for all those sacrifices by which the Word with love has been made accessible to me.

The cross in our lives is difficult to bear. It seldom looks like what we expect. It is seldom convenient, fair or pleasant. We even allow our faith to become tattered. The resurrection of faith for the mending processes is what this book is about. The struggle for faith leads to a faith equal to all struggles, to a revival of health in spirit that is most enduring against overwhelming odds. After threshing about with dismal loads and sinking into despair, human creatures long to discover how their lives are firmly grounded in the eternal, in Jesus and His love. The forces of health can be given new freedom when His love reduces antagonisms and renews distinctions long left muddled or blurred.

Whether we are behind bars of prison or the bars of discouragement, confined in hospital wards or bad marriages—wherever we may find ourselves a failure or in ceaseless pain and hardship—our human spirit flickers as we let the Lord touch us in our hearts. We are restless till we rest in Him. Our hearts need mending till we commend them to Him.

The challenge to religious faith may be more or less avoided until our adversity enlarges. Trained to be increasingly self-reliant, persons in most cultures tend toward self-trust. This book offers a statement in behalf of trust in *God* and its consequent healing power. "When I am afraid, I put my trust in thee. In God, whose word I praise, in God I trust without a fear" *(Psalm 56:3,4)*.

James Hefley wrote of the life of Rochunga Pudaite, faithful founder of Bibles for the World Incorporated. In this article in *Moody Monthly* in 1973, the great missionary leader is quoted explaining the nature of faith in this way: "You can stretch this band," he said, referring to a rubber band looped across his fingers, "only to a certain point. But faith never breaks from stretching. The more you stretch it, the stronger it becomes." Here is the secret of spiritual renewal in mending the brokenhearted. My hope is that this book may be of help to those who would dare to act with this kind of trust in their journeys under strain.

—Richard Kaiser

Contents

1. **THROUGH SURRENDER** 15
   No Exemption from Burdens ... God's Infinite Love ... The Secret of Surrender ... Pride Must Go ... The Freedom of Surrender ... The Urgency of Surrender ... The Beauty of Surrender ... The Illumination of Surrender ... Misguided Strivings? ... The Real Choices ... Phony Repudiations ... Willful Pride ... Demoralizing Doubts ... New Perspectives ... The Yielded Will

2. **THROUGH A LIFE OF DEVOTION** ..39
   Our Most Important Choices ... True Obedience ... Trusting God ...Our Spiritual Privileges ... The Enlarging Life ... The Habit of Devotion ... The New Birth ... Christ's Probing Questions ... The Danger of Comparisons ... Life's Tug-Of-Wars ... Our Inner Attitudes ... Personal Inventory ... New Images ... From Crisis to Privilege ... Values and Choices ... Renewal Through Christ

3. **THROUGH SUFFERING** 63
   Understanding Suffering... Purifying Attitudes ... The Lesson of Living ... Understanding Myself ... The Answer to Ignorance ... Knowing Who We Are ... Conquering Through Christ ... Purpose Provides Therapy ... Losing Heart and Gaining Hope ... Meaning in Christ ... Answers to Our Torments ... Knowing the Love of God ... God's Communications ... The Blockage of Pride ... Questions and Answers ... Begin with Faith

4. **THROUGH SERVICE** 85

    Christian Faith at Work ... Limited Outlooks ... Affirming True Faith ... Be Helped by Helping ... Coming Home to Reality ... Sacrifice at Work ... Our Inner Adversaries ... Distortions of Self ... Three Secrets for Mending ... From Self to Others ... Redemption and Forgiveness ... Warped Cultural Values ... True Trust in God

5. **THROUGH LOVE AND JOY** 105

    The Power of Faith ... New Attitudes Through Faith ... New Outlooks and Goals ... Learn to Love Again ... The Danger of Aberrations ... The Humbling Steps ... Understanding Clearly ... Pleasure Versus Love and Joy ... Mending Through Love and Joy ... The Shape of Love ... Love in Action ...The Test of Faith ... The Joy of the Lord ... Fulfillment in Christ

The Mending Heart

1

Through Surrender

> *He glows forever in all consciousness;*
> *Forgiveness, love, and hope possess the pit,*
> *And bring our endless guilt, like shadow's bars.*
> —Delmore Schwartz

Have you ever tried to capture a grasshopper out in the weeds, or gone chasing after a flitting butterfly as it dips and weaves just beyond your grasp? Just when you think you have your prey, you end up empty-handed!

The elusiveness of victory and joy in life is a common experience for all of us. Many of us are able to define or describe our concepts of victory and joy, but others of us us are less sure—we may dwell only on our pains, losses and struggles, nevertheless being sure that "there must be a better way!" Most of us will agree that there must be some way to fill the gap between what we face in brokenness and what we dream of having and being.

We as human beings do appear fragile, if studied under a certain light. We collapse under all kinds and degrees of burdens, both real and imagined. We can lose our vigor, our morale, our hope. We hardly wear elephant-hides; instead, our sensitivities make us penetrable, our vanities leave us vulnerable. With thin skins and fantasies we complicate our problems in life.

What we are evolves so much from what we *aim for*, and from the composite thought patterns that we construct from the past. How we *think* is largely determined by our hierarchy of valued ideas. And these ideas differ in their priority and in their degree of usefulness in identifying and solving real problems in our lives.

This means that what really counts in how we live our lives is what we *put first*. We are not as fragile as we sometimes seem to be. The Christian is a person who has the privilege of exemplifying just what robustness a human being possesses. Human hardiness is a state of mind and soul. The Christian's strength in mind and soul is rooted in Jesus Christ.

The renowned Scottish theologian William Barclay states simply the case for the Christian:

> . . . Jesus Christ is the atmosphere in whom the Christian lives . . . The Christian is never unaware of the presence of Jesus Christ; he never forgets that Jesus Christ is the spectator of all that he does and the hearer of all that he says; he never thinks of himself as attempting or approaching any task alone; . . . His whole life is linked inseparably to the risen and the living and the ever-present Christ . . .[1]

Here clearly is the priority, the desire that brings about strength. The Christian has an abiding connection with Christ.

No Exemption from Burdens

The Christ-immersed person will hardly be free from aches and burdens. Do you know anyone not bearing burdens? Do you know anyone free from wretchedness, defeat or losses? Life for most of us includes some shattering events that are not convenient or temporary in their timing. The entire process of living with a physical body in a dangerous physical world involves severe risk.

Can you take a vacation trip along freeways without significant risk? Can you strive for good results in your work without incurring some real threat? When do hazards ever leave our bodies, our homes, our schools and work sites, our streets, our communities and our whole environment? Risks and pains in many forms are everywhere—an inescapable condition.

Suppose a family is bearing the load of cystic fibrosis in the daughter, who can only anticipate great limitations and early death. Resentments may smolder in the family members, and also in neighbors and friends. Any one of them might easily say, "This load is unfair!" This sample of life may lead any one of them to despair and to avoidance of God. Where indeed can there be joy in days and nights filled with this kind of misery?

Think of the grief besetting a family with meager income, or one where a parent loses employment after 27 years of faithful service, or of a home snarled in the agonies of alcoholism. Where has all the goodness gone? Where are the rewards and victories of which all earlier dreams were made? The occasions for *mending* are countless. And yet repair cannot be foreseen.

If you lift your eyes to look farther afield, you will likely see only more massive heartache around this earth. In addition to the continuing poverty, the famine and droughts, there will be the sequences of floods, earthquakes, wars, storms and disease.

Though remote from your doorstep, incalculable anguish is being felt somewhere by many people. How can this be repaired?

God's Infinite Love

The infinitude of God's love is a starting place for each person. The Christ-connected persons have the obligation of representing and declaring this Good News. You want to counter discouragement to conquer despair. You want to diminish futility, fright and depression. You would like to restore yourself and others. The Christian in history can share insights about the mending process by which God brings relief to those under trial.

Elton Trueblood has offered three considerations which evolve from God's love: 1) to know that whatever we lose we can feel grateful for what we have already had; 2) to know that we consciously strive to bear out in our lives the quality of that which has been lost; 3) to know that one's own personal misery can be reduced or glorified by being shared.[2] There is indeed relief in the human sense from fixing on the abundance of love and fellowship with the past and with the present. In the simple facts of this knowledge one derives light, and some of the shadows can be lifted. The sense of responsibility, nourished by evidence of love and concern by others, becomes a repair unit in a person. Trueblood ovserved that "the best of healing medicine is not time, but *sharing*."[3]

The Christian believer draws from a commitment in depth to the majesty and power of Jesus. "For we did not follow cleverly devised myths when we made known to you the power and coming of our Lord Jesus Christ, but we were eyewitnesses of his majesty" *(2 Peter 1:16)*. When we are broken in heart, we can do well to measure the message of Saint Paul: "But, I say, walk by the Spirit, and do not gratify the desires of the flesh" *(Galatians 5:16)*. When we are about to yield to capture by depression, we can stand fast and not submit to the slavery of lost hope.

The Secret of Surrender

The issue has been set in these terms: *we are all to become captives; the crucial question is—captives to the Lord, or captives to the temptations and the torment of this world?* Where, when, how and to what shall we surrender? Let us consider the last part of this question first.

To what should we surrender? The Lord Jesus Christ is the answer. Yielding to Him requires confession of His primacy, His power and His will. It is in this confession that a person begins a restorative process by turning away from the self-serving primacy of pride, intellect and flesh. For those deep in tragedy or stresses of pain, this confession psychologically signifies a turning around from the ache toward the Master. In fact, it is a simple communication acknowledging who and what shall master the senses.

Surrendering oneself to God through the Savior is a declaration of the sacredness of this life. It is an affirmation of love to the Source of live and love. Psychologists and medical healers attest to the power of love and faith in restoring the infirmed. Putting oneself into Christ is putting oneself into the Spirit to allow for the powerful forces of love in bringing rescue and renewal. The great battles of tension that take place in both diseased and tormented tissues can be touched with miraculous relief just by infusion of *caring love*. Even in those cases where the tissue ceases to function, the person *in Christ* has known His strong intervention.

Pride Must Go

Often the aspiring Christian will be a person who wishes to honor God but does not wish to give up pride and certain appetites or habits. Like a skier attempting to pass around both sides of a tree at once, one may nominally avow God, but not by admitting to either sin or renounced self. This is somewhat like the bigamist avowedly committed to two spouses: "I am doing no wrong—and besides, I love them both the same!"

Breaking the habit of pride can be as difficult as chipping away at concrete with a straw. Pride is a blindness. Under its effects many of us are unable to discern our true magnitude of weakness. We tend to protect our pride even more vigorously than we might our own bodies. But in the confession to Christ there is a falling away of pride. When you compare yourself to Him and His life, in that instant you see! When in place of demonic idols, man-centered standards and self-centered cravings, you set your life beside that of Christ and beside God's holiness, pride slips away and you see your crime against love and noble human efforts.

The surrendering Christian is becoming a mending Christian. Could we know darkness without the sense of sight and light? Could we truly grasp our ignoble ways without comparison with the purity of the Lord? When we yield to God and Jesus in repentance, not only will grace touch us in our needs, but also we convert certain attitudes which break the chains of our egocentric predicament. This refers to the predicament of an individual to perceive things only in terms of how they affect him or her. The consequence of this condition often is to be less capable of forming objective impressions, of seeing the reality in life's events. Mending can proceed as this psychological delusion dissolves under the effect of surrender and under the effect of acknowledging the Lord.

The Freedom of Surrender

Where should we surrender? The surrender of self to God and His Son appears somewhat like the freedom granted to one in praying; it can happen almost anywhere. Douglas Steere has said of prayer, "In learning to pray, no laboratory is needed but a room; no apparatus but ourselves."[4] Our broken hearts are probably sufficient determiners of an appropriate place for repentance. It may even be that, since our struggles and confusions are ruptures of our wholeness, we should seek conciliation wherever the conflicts are rampant.

It must be noted that conciliation is often enhanced by an *intermediary*. The processes of healing antagonists do better when they include some other person as catalyst. You may find your repentance first coming when you are alone. For many others, however, confession may be facilitated in the personal presence of, and through conversation with, a valued person like a friend, a priest or pastor, a counselor or a family member. The truly important fact is that you can turn to Jesus in the midst of other functions.

Christian surrender is a form of binding the self to Jesus. Thus the location is unimportant in a sense. This is a deep-sighing kind of *real change*. It may occur while playing badminton, or on a crowded ferry, or at a concert, or in one's room or car. What truly counts is that there be *spiritual change* in the heart and soul. Binding represents a behavioral contract with the Lord. The changes produced by this contract are those of a new peace, and their site of occurrence is best chosen by you and by me.

The Urgency of Surrender

When should we surrender? Much has been said in mild disdain of those who get "foxhole religion." The implication in such judgments is that this route to faith is somehow an inferior way to come to God. But it is grossly unfair to mock the human tendency to wait until the last minute in asking for help.

The truth is that Jesus sent his preachers to where people were—*to wherever they were*. Some of us become hearers only in the din of threat. Some of us resist kneeling until the hazards about and within us have grown to enormous proportions. The timing of Christian submission knows no set formula or specification. It sometimes takes rough-and-tumble distresses to prepare a person for humbling.

This universe permits great freedoms. Even those who profess worship of God and Christ drift off in meandering ways. Other interests increase, so that church, faith and God receive scant attention. Those of us with this tendency get closer to being alleged Christians than we can likely detect. We need the conversion almost as much as the pagan, but we don't know it. But whether it be a first confession or a reconfession of Christ, the timing is likely to be individualized. Putting oneself in Christ will depend upon grace and one's convergence of needs.

A beautiful testimony of encouragement may be found in a tiny book by the late Quaker philosopher Rufus Jones, entitled *The Double Search*.[5] Jones wrote of a famous myth in Plato's *Symposium,* a myth saying that primitive man was round, had four hands and four feet, and had one head with two faces looking opposite ways. The myth continues that, because of his fleetness and skill in rolling over and going anywhere he wished, "the round person" was such a threat to the power of Zeus that each man had to be cut in two.

Jones used this myth to introduce the idea of two halves of an original which forever longed to be united. In Christian faith the divine other, God, is seeking us just as we search for Him. Religion for Jones includes the two pillars, *atonement* and *prayer*. God offers deliverance from a life of sin, and this deliverance can be ours through our positive yielding of will. We can be comforted that God is enduring in His quest for us; as we choose to renounce our meandering ways with a timing defying prediction, we may find His peace and strength as near as our confessional prayer.

24/The Mending Heart

The Beauty of Surrender

How should we surrender? Oh, what variations there are in how to do most things in religion! The social gospel leaders oppose notions of the individual gospel preachers; those who believe in the fundamental business of being "changed" or "born in the Spirit" may be ignored or disdained by intellectualized, ecclesiastical scholars. Whether you are a charismatic or a noncharismatic believer of Jesus, whether you are comfortable with the idea of sin or not, you will likely have an ego that prevents personal victory over self.

Norman Vincent Peale has signaled out the element of fear that accompanies so much of our lives.[6] Peale cited his own personal progress with (and need for) skill in letting God take over. The act of surrendering, in Peale's view, is an act of *deliberate mental giving up to God.* This involves decision, then honest admission of inadequacy, then submission through declaration. In effect, *one yields both self and problems to God through Jesus.*

Dr. Peale has shared the story of how he found the hitherto-denied peace of God's grace and power. After years of feeling inadequate for his duties, having spent days in negative thinking and conversation with his wife while on vacation, he followed his wife's request to pray in these terms: "Dear Lord, I now give myself, my life, my mind, my body, my soul to You. I give You all my fears. If You want me to fail, I am willing to accept failure. Whatever You do with me is all right with me. Take all of me. I surrender everything to You."[7] The immediacy, the intensity, the magnitude of Peale's relief gave him the certainty of God's healing presence.

Another "how-to" prayer of confession has been used by countless thousands over the earth: "I am convinced by God's Word that I am a lost sinner. I believe that Jesus Christ died for sinners and shed His blood to put away my sins. I NOW receive Him as my personal Lord and Savior, and will by His help confess Him before men."

In these two versions of declaring one's allegiance to God is the simple, though essential, unhooking from self. It is the necessary prelude to the humble commission of self to God. This is surrender in the Christian sense.

But we know that surrender is more—it is a shedding of inhibitions, a removing of veils. It is a psychospiritual simplifying process. It is a taming and rededication. It is the beginning of a whole, ever-enlarging foundation in faith.

Christian surrender is the means for committing oneself to the power and directives of Jesus. We surrender when we make Christ the Resurrection and the Life for ourselves and over our lives in sin. That is the plain, simple truth. We may not understand how we could have been dead so long in sin; we only know the deep inward blessing of His presence in giving us a mended heart and spirit. He can bring us to life, just as He did for Lazarus in the tomb at Bethany *(John 11:44)*. Surrendering is how we affirm our belief in Him and yield to Him.

The Illumination of Surrender

Another perspective should be added in considering surrender, that of *illumination*. Surrender is

26/The Mending Heart

a time of breakthrough and breakdown. As you collapse your defenses and vanities, your resistances and fears, you feel the brightness of new light. Saul who became Paul recounts his own experience just prior to receiving the baptism from Ananias. In reporting to King Agrippa, he said, "At midday, O king, I saw on the way a light from heaven, brighter than the sun, shining round me . .. I heard a voice saying to me in the Hebrew language, 'Saul, Saul, why do you persecute me? It hurts you to kick against the gods" (Acts 26:13, 14). Under the force of shame, we see here the onset of illumination in a person resistant to the yoke. We see contrariness to the unmatched dawning of truth.

This contrariness comes with a certain amount of tension. William Blake phrased it this way: "Without contraries is no progression." Out of our tensions comes the response of new vision.

Christianity if a forceful, therapeutic, heart-mending power when we immerse ourselves in it through Christ. The Christ-centered effects can be lost in the church; for many people shrink from the idea of sin, from the gospel of conviction, redemption, atonement and salvation. But through surrender and resurrender we come simply to be ourselves, unvarnished and unpretentious.

James Thurber is reported to have said, "The proper study of mankind is man, says man." It is this kind of self-centering by which we construct the many pretenses of our personalities. You and I grow up in a culture which rewards our ability to bluff. We are praised when we "put on" or successfully adopt certain artificialities to go along with being a hard competitor. We are pushed thoroughly and for sound practical reasons to gain independence. Before too long we come to believe in our own glory and to admire our own talents. It is easy to go from *studying* self to *worshipping* self without realizing the process. We grow fond of self, and we learn to never admit weakness.

Misguided Strivings?

This learning of bluff and autonomy joins with another human trait—the tendency to strive for the sake of striving. While we find substantial advantages in being a vigorous, ever-aspiring pursuer of goals, our senses become dulled in this habit of prizing struggle. Blaise Pascal observed, "The struggle alone pleases us, not the victory . . . In disputes we like to see the clash of opinions, but not at all to contemplate truth when found . . . We never seek things for themselves, but for the search."[8] We get so enamored with change, anticipation and the future of what is to come next that we lose the capacity to savor the real present.

It is this *striver's ethic* which in part impedes surrender to God. We become locked into a kind of thought which dictates attention to what comes after our secular victories. The world's values crowd out those of God. To a large degree the world's standards replace those of God, especially where they require a choice to be made. It becomes difficult to be Christian in a pre-Christian age.

Being Christian in eighteenth-century England posed hazards for the esteemed Romantic poet, William Blake. Men of philosophy and science presented very awesome attacks for thinkers in Blake's age who adhered to a Christian stance. It was not easy to be popular (perhaps then or now) when contending that the crisis of civilizaton was the threat of dissolution by failing to heed the Jesus in each person.[9] The Christian faith tends to lift one aside from the world while requiring continuing involvement with it. The differences which emerge in experience and conduct may separate Christian from non-Christian at times, but Christians are hardly called to be mere recluses.

The Real Choices

Surrender to God through confession and affirmation in no way demands a retreat out of the world. Instead, it leads ultimately to *choices in the world*. Some Christians devoutly express their faith by virtually total renunciation and monastic isolation. But a more challenging response is that of Christians who continue striving for service to and with people where they are, boldly committed in faith and firmly rooted in desire to serve the Savior's cause.

Those wo have been forced to decide between agonizingly attractive alternatives, like the child who can have *either* an ice cream cone *or* a trip to the park, but not both—know the strain of making clear, simple Christian choices at times. In Sophocles' play *Antigone* we see how tough it can be to decide between manmade law and inwardly interpreted divine law. As long as a person stays in the world among the most human, physical and real social circumstances, conflicts of conscience will add to the challenges of being Christian. In the lives of many people such an onslaught of both large and small conflicts represents a part of what they feel as bewilderment.

Anyone who works with people and observes their conduct or listens to their concerns will soon recognized the prevalence of personal anxiety and stresses. There is a weariness from discord, a bewilderment from conflicts, and often a very serious temporary loss of hope. It is by this hopelessness that *meanings* seem to drain away.

"Where have all the flowers gone?" This plaintive question captures some of the discouragement felt by those with a broken or lost sense of meaning. In many fields of medicine, religion and psychology we continue learning about interwoven dimensions of disease and of healing, of breakdown and rehabilitation. In many cases the ailments of body tissues are linked with ailments of mind and spirit, and the wholeness of a person's health is increasingly recognized. Helping in the recovery of meanings may be a part of therapeutic counsel rendered by almost all health-care professionals, whatever may be their specific case of disability, whatever may be the immediate symptoms with which they are confronted.

Phony Repudiations

The surrendering-to-God process, the first step in our thesis here, is a positive act. Unfortunately, there are many barriers which people employ to hold themselves from this act. One barrier to surrender is repudiation of the Christian church on the grounds that it is either an archaic or a historically abusive institution. It is argued, for example, that the church is an outworn, useless remnant, one that has frequently been more harsh and inhumane than any ruthless dictator. Those who use this barrier emphasize the dismal and brutal conditions wrought through and by the church in history. They will admit to being more than perplexed; they will state their conviction that religion through the church is more an evil than a moral asset.

This honesty of the protester, however, hardly justifies mute response from Christian believers. It is good to encourage this expression of real disdain. After all, God's church has, through man's weakness, been the source of imperative, dogmatic and inhumane abuse. The ordinary people in the church have not perfectly or humanely shed themselves of grievous inconsistencies. Worshippers of God have indeed been guilty of harmful sins—and still may be. In admitting this factual picture of the church, one is no doubt likely to be able to widen the focus on the repudiators to consider how the Christian influence began to stimulate awareness of great mistakes and injustices, of corruptions in society and in the church and in persons.

With a widening focus, this kind of resister might be led to study people like Saint Francis and John Wesley, who valiantly sensitized society to its iniquities. One peephole version of Christianity may then permit the repudiator to add understanding of the broader human situation and of Christ's people imperfectly at work in commitment to a righteous God.

Willful Pride

A second barrier to surrender to God is pride. This condition is often masked behind resentment of authority. We have reached an age in which many have come to like their fredom from discipline, from reminders of moral standards and authority. We have certainly enlarged the importance of being independent, of concealing our needs for help, and of shunning moral judgments of others.[10] We may turn to opiates, mood-enhancing drugs and frenzied forms of recreation for seeking escape from stress; but in many cases we are too proud to demolish our own opposition to God.

God can become so gradually unimportant as we glut ourselves on any of our successes or riches that we really become deluded! We see ourselves as being the source of our own strength. In some degree we take self as an idol to be prized and worshipped. Then, our pride grows to enormity. We fail to sense how our self-importance makes difficult any thought of admitting weakness. Certainly *sin* is not to be confessed! After all, our thinking may go, we are too superior to be guilty of any significant wrong. Pride leads us to minimize or to dismiss grievances, hurts or violations of moral law. "I may not be angelic," I may say, "but my conduct is better than most, and I resent anyone implying that I'm a sinner."

This barrier blocks surrender to the Creator because of self-adoration and leads to self-blindness. For example, my greed, or my jealousy or my envy might fire off volleys of hostile comments to my family, or customers or vendors without my detecting how much torment is being produced by my love of self. This kind of pride is at times more impervious than an armor-plate. Any honest observer must admit that proud Christians all too easily bar awareness of their own needs and faults.

Demoralizing Doubts

A third barrier to Christian surrender, the confusion produced by three kinds of observations, leaves certain people with doubts: 1) they are puzzled by the prosperity of people who ignore (indeed often reject) all God-reference and divine power; 2) they are puzzled by people who claim religious fervor but clearly act in hypocisy; 3) they are puzzled by what they perceive as inequities in the way God grants healing, health and joy to some persons while allowing wretchedness and agonies to others. These observations create a predicament, and they block spiritual surrender.

The person who is earnest in desiring to serve his God and fellowman will soon find a way to counter this predicament. This person finds that greater devotional study and spiritual thought are necessary if these kinds of observations are not to hold him in confusion. This is the person who presses on in search of more than partial truth. The church is recognized as a body of imperfect aspirants whose conduct will at times contradict Christ's teachings. But a greater truth about true Christians must be sought through meditations and study.

New Perspectives

Anyone who meditates and prays, together with intensive study of the Bible and of great Christian authors, is bound to discover new perspectives on these questions of apparent inequities, injustices and fanaticisms. It becomes more clear, for example, that Jesus was not leading people to expect great worldly treasures through their discipleship. He was not urging people to compare enviously their storehouses with those of others. The great truth appears that religious motives pulsate the new life by which wrongs are righted. The Bible continues to offer that source of hope through which all kinds of stumbling human beings are beginning to feel new balance and direction.

Another valuable perspective unfolds around the shallow judgment of the hypocrisy that may be found in Christians. This judgment affords a rather convenient excuse for those who wish for an excuse, but the real differences between Christians and non-Christians are highlighted through careful study. The idea becomes clear that Christians subordinate themselves to the Lord while also attempting to honor His Word in loving service to mankind. The myth is dispelled that Christ's followers are already free from sins and unkind behavior. Christians are not super-people, nor are they yet flawless. But sensitive study will bring the insight that Christians are an endeavoring fellowship that strives to oppose sins and to bring social witness of God's healing powers.

More difficult to handle is the observation, singled out by many, that God leaves numerous tragic hardships for certain persons and dispenses joyful relief to others in a way that is grotesquely unfair. We are so steeped in the practice of being critical (it is a part of practical everyday living) that our intelligence leads us to the point of judging God. With this criticism set in place and blocking faith, surrender to God seems foolish. *What we will* continues to take precedence over *seeking His will*. We must be led beyond bitter efforts to prosecute God to *knowing God firsthand in experience*. The meditating person in this way goes beyond knowing *about* God. With Job this person might experience the living Lord in an abiding trust which dissolves this barrier *(Job 42:2-6)*. It is in *this experience* that surrender then occurs.

The heart of surrender, a part of the redemptive process, is the process of being born again. Gerald Heard has provided an incisive analysis of surrender in likening it to the special quality of a child. For Heard the child's openness, innocence and wonder are only symptoms of a deeper condition, which Heard cites as "a certain quality of consciousness itself."[11] This is a quality of looking at the world not as something to be exploited, but of admitting that we in ourselves have nothing, that we have lost our way and have need of God's inexhaustible power.

The Yielded Will

As we reach out toward the inseparable connection with Jesus, of which we found Barclay speaking, we find the psychospiritual acknowledgment that Christians make in subordinating their selves and their wills. Here, they find, is their first victory in bridging that void between brokenness and dreams. With the spirit of God touching their wounds and soothing their hurts, they feel the Lord's relief. This inward transformation, wholly incomparable, captures the elusive victory more human than all selfish conquests.

One of the great (though somewhat obscure) reformers of the seventeenth century, Benjamin Whichcote, wrote of this transforming power in these terms: "With God there cannot be reconciliation without our becoming God-like . . . God is more inward to us than our own souls . . ."[12] Knowing the self to be only in God through Jesus is sure strength for all burdens. Repentance shatters the shackle of the self separated from God. His loving strength prevails, and mending can proceed.

The problems of the human heart and spirit (unfortunately, it seems) are problems of fickleness. We can be mended, but we deviate and meander in ways that repeat our errors. Our attentiveness can and does lapse. In God's grace we may receive forgiveness and new life, only to discover that we have continuing need for discipline. Our road to Christ through surrender is rather difficult for most of us. Even if we are sensitized to God while asleep, we tend too easily to drift away when we are awake (Psalm 16:7). The sovereignty of God needs the refreshment of renewed surrender if a life of devotion is to grow. How much more realistic for us to think not of being *mended* but instead of *mending*—to mark indelibly our continuing need to submit to His yoke.

36/The Mending Heart

1. William Barclay, *Turning to God* (Grand Rapids: Baker Book House, 1972), p. 60.
2. Elton Trueblood, *The Life We Prize* (New York: Harper & Row, 1951),pp. 184-86.
3. Ibid., p. 187.
4. Douglas Steere, *Dimensions of Prayer* (New York: Women's Division of Christian Service, The Methodist Church, 1962), p. 6.
5. Rufus Jones, *The Double Search* (Richmond, Indiana: Friends United Press, reprint of 1960 edition by J.C. Winston, Philadelphia, 1975).
6. Norman Vincent Peale, *Positive Thinking for a Time Like This* (Englewood Cliffs, New Jersey: Prentice Hall, 1961, 1975), p. 42.
7. Ibid., pp. 44-46.
8. Blaise Pascal, *"Pensees" and "The Provincial Letters"* (New York: Modern Library, 1941), pp. 47-48.
9. Victor N. Paananen, *William Blake* (Boston: Twayne Publishers, 1977), p. 154.
10. William Barclay, *By What Authority* (Valley Forge: Judson Press, 1975), pp. 205, 210.
11. Gerald Heard, *The Code of Christ* (New York: Harper & Bros., 1941), p. 71.
12. Benjamin Whichocote's Appendix to *Aphroisms* (1975) p. 13, and *Select Sermons* (1968), p. 109, cited in Rufus Jones, *Spiritual Reformers in the 16th & 17th Centuries* (Boston: Beacon Press, 1959), pp. 293, 296.

2

Through A Life Of Devotion

*Dear fellow-creature, praise our God of Love.
That we are so admonished, that no day
Of conscious trial be a wasted day.*

—*W. H. Auden*

One of the most gifted visionary landscape painters in American history was Thomas Cole. Though born in England, he drew from his deep love for the New England mountain wilderness to give impetus to a native school of landscape painting. It was Cole who once observed that the good of going into the mountains is that life is reconsidered. "Going into the mountains" can indeed bring new corrective perspectives to a person. Many of life's contrasts and relativities have a way of sorting themselves out when one is alone in the grandeur and space of a mountain retreat.

Christians have long sought and gained this kind of clarity from retreats for spiritual auditing. Certainly in the modern Western world most people are caught up in varying degrees of frenzy. The space and crowding of events prohibit the privacy of considering the meanings and direction of living. All too often those who need mending cannot find the conditions which nuture and restore the soul. It is a tragic truth that people under continuing burdens often allow thier spiritual life to weaken. It is more than irony that they give up first what they need the most.

Our Most Important Choices

Nearly, fifty years ago William Pepperell Montague wrote, "The momentous question is whether the things we care for most are at the mercy of the things we care for least."[1] One of the ways in which we compound our plight, whether it be spiritual, physical or mental, is that of making choices which have worsening consequences. The alcoholic all too easily keeps on going to those places and thinking those thoughts which continue the domination of alcohol in his days and nights. Those who suffer strong fears or intense hatreds often persist in choosing actions geared to continuing their deep tensions. Often our tastes lead on to self-indulgences that we know only worsen our predicaments. Sensual pleasures and cravings for power sometimes roll on to dominate our choices, making our frustrations more grave and creating more anguish. It is *in spite* of our knowledge that we tend to sacrifice real treasures in our lives for the sake of experiences which prove sooner or later to be trivial.

We seem to be conditioned to doing one of two things with our religious devotion, neither of which is helpful in mending our brokenness. One thing is the tendency to acquire and use devotion as we might an exercise machine, namely, *infrequently*. Like an item placed away in the attic or cellar, devotion remains largely overlooked. A second way, perhaps just as common, is the tendency to use devotion as we would a bandage, namely, *in emergencies*. In each case we have examples of religious devotion being potentially helpful for a little while, but without the promise of more lasting change. In these cases we are not living our devotion, we are just putting it on temporarily. But Christian faith must be far more than a put on if it is to make a difference in the health of our whole lives.

When we surrender to God through Christ and genuinely desire to become His followers, we will rejoice if we are able to live more committedly, more reverently in virtually all functions and moments. What is meant by an *enlarging devotional life?* What are some of the vital attributes of *spiritual devotion in Christ?* Such questions require several answers for those who would strive to be equipped for mending.

True Obedience

One of the most compelling qualities of Christian devotion is the *obedience* required. Just finding the means for reconsidering life as it transpires calls for *discipline*. Just attending to the moral standards of Christianity calls for *concentration*. Just holding to the real presence and power of Jesus calls for *priority*. We know that we cannot thread a needle without focus and rigorous concentration. So too, if we are to thread our way to His path, we must obey His calling.

Christian compliance is a form of yoking, a centerpoint of faith, "Blessed are those who have not seen and yet believe" *(John 20:29)*. In our efforts to elevate belief in the Lord as part of a life of devotion, we clarify our awareness of where He is and of our relation to Him. From recent psychological research we learn that in animals there are not only single cells in the brain that respond to where the animal is, but that there are also different kinds of these spatial-orientation cells. These cells at different locations perform different functions, enabling the animal to *organize* information about details of location in space.

Obedience to God must issue from a comparable kind of spiritual organization to God. Obedience may in part involve development of "knowledge" maps which increase the importance of our "knowing" relationship to God. Unwavering obedience may really mean improving our ability to keep God as our divine reference point.

Trusting God

Another compelling attribute of dedicated followers of Christ is *trust*. Trusting God is more than some occasional afterthought; it is more than one or two threads in the garment we wear on certain days; it is more than a nominal affirmation of a religious creed uttered quarterly. Trust must come to a prevailing position of domination in our consciousness—and it can! Those who seek healing embody in their whole feeling this commitment to the Creator as they go forward from conversion to unrestricted confidence in His power and loving concern.

You know the trust you feel in your banker, for example, or in the bridge over which you regularly drive. You know your trust in the brakes of your automobile, a trust implicit in the movements you make and the choices you render in traffic. Psychologically, trust is a form of dependence, an expression of reliance. In living a life of devotion, Christians live this trust more emphatically. It fuses with their love of God, with their surrender to Him.

Our trust in God is reciprocated; He trusts us too. Devoted Christians who are led by God in turn receive the strength to lead others. Paul's assurance to Corinthians shows this trust: "Blessed be the God and Father of our Lord Jesus Christ, the Father of mercies and God of all comfort, who comforts us in all our affliction, so that we may be able to comfort those who are in any affliction, with the comfort with which we ourselves are comforted by God" *(2 Corinthians 1:3, 4)*. Just as people respond to minimal cues (provided by split-second presentation of stimuli) to leap to highly confident conclusions, thoughtfully devoted Christians leap from their own brief gifts of comfort to solid conclusions of faith. These conclusions of faith in turn serve as a springboard for sending forth comforts to others in peril.

God's trust of us is signalled by the freedom to choose or not to choose responding to His Word. This is unique trust, granted to no other creature. As part of our increasing trust in the Lord, as part of our mending, we are to receive the Cross—our own. Of this devotion William Hocking once wrote: "Its way to happiness is the path of a will to create in love, which is inseparable from a will to create through suffering."[2] We are offered no escape from problems, no waiver of pains, but we mend as we learn how our duty leads on to love and wholeness.

Our Spiritual Privileges

We must note a third attribute of Christians living in devotion. It is the insight of our *privileges*. From heightened sensitivity to God comes the special glimpse of God's love and concern for all of us, including our neighbors. The weight of His concern shines in, if only for brief moments, to show us the weight of our obligation to others. C.S. Lewis in a most beautiful insight described how we are all day long, in some degree, *privileged* to help one another either toward honor and dignity or toward disgusting dishonor.[3] Lewis uses his description to urge awe upon us for the enormity of this privilege, saying, "There are no *ordinary* people. You have never talked to a mere mortal . . . Next to the Blessed Sacrament itself, your neighbor is the holiest object presented to your senses."[4]

Here we have one of the durable sinews of health in the whole of human existence. Seeing the bona fide worth in persons and seeing their possibilities contingent upon *our* treatment of them—this perceptual attitude can withstand all kinds of torment and disappointment. In a movingly simple recall of what he had once said and thought on Good Friday, while in the unbearable pison camp on the River Kwai, Ernest T. Gorden wrote, "By his death he gave to men the responsibility of caring for one another and doing his Father's will; to sons and mothers and fathers and brothers and sisters he assigned the task of caring for all other sons and mothers and fathers and brothers and sisters. No small commission."[5]

Sometimes in spiritual life a person dwindles to

almost zero. One may feel such bitterness against his troubles that there is little room left for anything else. The heart in this way closes under despair or deep resentments. Often one repels any overture of kindness or indeed any reference to Jesus Christ; he or she seems bound to reject the Word in whatever form it may be offered. But the power of God begins in small steps to soften this callus, to stimulate new wonderment, new peace and possibly new invitations. God's agents (whoever might be drawn to be His messenger) remain steadfast in reaching out to the mending heart and in responding to the sense of commission cited by Lewis. If Gordon could discover the sense of privilege for himself deep in a rotting jungle prison, surely we may expect to find our own pure sense of love wherever we are.

The Enlarging Life

An enlarging devotional life in Christ girds us with strength to obey God, with reliance upon Him. It gives us the sense of privilege in knowing His true love through ourselves for others. This is the point: *our renewal is in itself our own mending.* Living a life of devotion signifies a new concept of one's whole life as an act of obedience to God. This is what is meant by commitment. It means putting the whole mind and soul in Christ.

Yes, we can become almost constantly aware of Jesus' presence. Our thinking, our motives, our outlooks can be infused with His priority in all that we are and all that we do. Our valued ideas all come to be guided by Him.

46/The Mending Heart

Over thirty years ago an American navigator, in charge of determining a lost plane's course in the black emptiness of Pacific Ocean skies at night, chose to attempt a calculation based only on two faint stars and the North Star, Polaris. His plane was without radio contact, without any visual contact with air and ground units. An added burden was the fact that the plane, designed for land-based operations, had been designed with *barely minimal* capacity to reach Honolulu. Determining the plane's actual course, and plotting what ought to be the course were this navigator's responsibilities. Heightened concern for the very limited fuel supply added to his grimness in making the right decisions.

He was well-trained in using a sextant for "shooting the stars," though inexperienced in its use under life-and-death conditions. The overcast sky allowed him to identify two stars doubtfully. Only the North Star shined bright and certain. Prayerfully, in the darkness of the craft (for it was without lights), he made his triangular "shot" three times, and then made the choice of course to be followed. Commitment and trust! A choice made in faith, a response to God's will, leading in that case to the joy of finally spotting and reaching the landing strip outside Honolulu—with ten minutes fuel supply remaining!

Living a life of Christian devotion means a pattern of constant choices in Christ. It means constant concern for fitting *means* to *ends*. Harry Emerson Fosdick once preached a sermon on the crucial problem of choosing the means by which we live and the ends for which we live. Choosing what we are living *for* in Christ leads us to commitment mentally and spiritually. It is this abiding commitment which makes all the difference in the means by which we live.

The Habit of Devotion

Have you thought about how many choices you make each waking day, and how many alternatives you have available in making them? Have you considered the *habit* you can introduce to virtually all your judgment situations? First, of course, you are judging much of the time what you think *about*. It may be the customer's need in front of you, and his disposition, which may lead you on to further choices and thoughts. Or it may be the long-term problem facing you in the household or at your work. Or it may be what you will do or say in the next meeting you are about to attend. How your mind makes those choices depends in large part on *what you put first*. The Christian is able to approach these moments with an awareness of Christ, with the habit of making these choices with Christ present.

With a need for a mending heart, can we do less than put Christ first by giving to Him a portion of our attention at all times? We have been told many times that what or how we speak comes from what we think, and that what we think comes from what is in our hearts. Living a devotional life in Christ surely calls us to behaving as if He were with us in all moments and transactions. Acquiring the *sense of devotional living* can grow as a mending process from this habit of thinking, feeling and willing to a priority position the *awareness of Christ at hand.*

The New Birth

Among the important features of devotionalism gaining control of one's whole life is that of new birth. Many Christians report feeling unparalleled freedom following surrender to the Lord. All classes and kinds of persons share a common experience in this feeling of new life. As former fears and inhibitions drop away, the newborn Christian feels a surging sense of release unlike any known before.

This devotionalism may spring forth with emotional liberation like that expressed in the multitudes of emigrants from Europe who settled in America in the late 1700s. They were diverse people who shortly after arrival in their new land experienced a bursting sense of nationalism. Henry Commager has analyzed this phenomenon to have been the result of these varied folks feeling *uniqueness* in their new freedom from old constraints.[7] Awakened to spaciousness and mobility, these men and women from the Old World forged ahead in a few decades to brand new conceptions and policies for living that would have been unthinkable in the old country. It is this vitality of new allegiance *and* of new creative forms that a devotionally inspired Christian shares with others born in Christ's Spirit.

A magnified discipline in devotion dispenses more consciousness of the Lord. One can say with ease silently, "Lord, I know you are with me now. Attend to my needs as I strive to act toward your purposes." This is the inward, deliberate heightening of awareness to God's guidance, a form of self-reminding that works! Periodic thoughts of Christ are not enough, though better than none at all. But for those hungering for relief from despair, Christian faith permits opening fully to the Holy Spirit in a constancy that submits one's individual will to that of Christ. George Buttrick has neatly underscored this kind of commitment with his account of Paul as a man who turned his back on peace rather than turning from Christ. Buttrick wrote, "Why? Because Christ had won his will . . .."[8]

This yielding of will may become a continuing meditation. Christ *does* make the difference—the difference between despair and hope, between dark futility and bright answers. Increasing one's time with Christ can hardly occur without patience, without listening or without solemn application of attention. There is a clarity that escapes many people in their modest efforts to attend to Jesus and His teachings. The values He would have us implement are often modified, especially as we grasp the fact that His values of human life are contrary to those which people ordinarily honor and seek. Meditation is thus an act taken to deepen this understanding of how Christ's values may both *require* and *lead to* changed conduct.

Christ's Probing Questions

The meditating Christian, however callous to the searching questions of self-attention, will be open to Christ's probing questions. Meditation, or reflection, is a process of self-discovery that most of us manage to elude. We almost succeed in keeping ourselves oblivious of our true selves, that part of our nature spurring us on to self-promotion. As long as we elude God's will by attending our own, we fail to incorporate Christ's revolutionary values. They are too "revolting," too self-diminishing for our tastes.

In the depths of predicament we can sometimes achieve the clarity by which to alter values. Such an insight, reported by Langdon Gilkey from his years in a Japanese Internment camp for civilians in North China, is similar to the insights experienced through meditation. Dr. Gilkey's report cites the captivity in which he saw people caught, the captivity of sin through self-love:

> In all of us, moreover, some power within seemed to drive us to promote our own interests against those of our neighbors. We were not our "true selves," the selves we wanted to be or liked to think we were.... Whenever we willed something, it was our own distorted will that did the willing, so that we could not will the good. Though quite free to will whatever we wanted to do in a given situation, we were not free to will to love others, because the will did not really want to.[9]

Inward deception, Dr. Gilkey went on to note, comes from fundamental self-concern of the total self as it functions from below our specific acts and thoughts. It is this self-concern that dictates and shapes our conduct out of harmony with the values of God. "The only hope in the human situation,"

Dr. Gilkey says, "is that the 'religiousness' of men finds its true center in God, and not in the many idols that appear in the course of our experience."[10] The person of real faith will indeed discern and claim in actual conduct that security and meaning are not in his own life but in the power and love of God. Meditation can bring that clarity required for this conversion from self-will to the will of God.

The Danger of Comparisons

To those many aspirants in the faith over the centuries there has been the danger of arriving at judgments of others who appear less committed to a life of devotion. As people center upon Christ, they are charged to avoid judging, and to acknowledge that all faithful followers will be traversing the path in their own ways, at their own pace. The sin of feeling good about one's own commitment is an ever-present hazard. The pride-habit rears up in even the most earnest follower of Christ.

Even more hazardous to those pressed into greater contemplation is the tendency to feel superior. With the secular habit of "succeeding" we have long joined the habit of designated superiority. One who succeeds is regarded as superior. No one could do more, however, to epitomize the inherent bad in the human creature than to allow this smugness to grow in the inward self, as one seeks indeed to remove it and other self-centered emotions. Finding oneself through attention upon Christ is a process that must proceed from beneath the shadows of self-satisfaction and judgment.

One's sense of unworthiness in meditation helps to certify that the quest of Jesus denies the irony of feeling either superiority or completion. The surrendered self is one that no longer thinks of self-accomplishment. Thinking about accomplishments is changed. The self is separated from the accomplishment; what is prized and is not *self* but *God's will being served*, God's purposes being achieved. Our selfish wills clash with God's will. As long as human wills predominate, there is anguish and strife. Just as meditating aids a person to break through delusions, so commitment to a life in Christ aids the healing of conflicts.

Life's Tug-of-Wars

Life's tug-of-wars go on for a lifetime. Most of us are hardheaded; we are resolute in preserving our pleasures, gains and freedoms. Those whom we observe to be "pious" don't inspire us to faith. Those whom we find to be the "big winners" in life may be indifferent to religious faith. So all too often we skirt around as many reminders of Christ's teachings as we can. We dismiss our inner pangs of Christian conscience, and we compound our real predicament by remaining more or less nominally believers without much rigor in devotion.

The emphasis upon inner rigor in devotion proves to be a means for one to view his own wisdom and will with caution. Buttrick wrote, "For the praying man learns to distrust his own wisdom."[11] So much of our whole cultural and educational inheritance nurtures the idea that we are to keep on straining for individual autonomy.

"What I make of myself is up to me. If I am to take a center-point anywhere, it should be in my own powers and competence." This is a widespread phenomenon of secular life, one that acts as a fountain to quench the thirst of self. Small wonder that the self becomes an idol!

Small wonder that we emphasize *what we do and gain* more than *what we construct spiritually*. Living a life of devotion brings no "prizes," earns few job promotions or accolades. It does, however, represent a choice in the direction of spiritual maturity. It does mean an effort to grow in becoming a source of encouragement and selfless justice. In the words of Elton Trueblood, "What we are is more significant, in the long run, than what we do."[12] From persistent devotional practices may emerge a person open to the disturber, Christ, a person empowered to inspire justice in and from others. The gifts of Christ's values to others may come best as we yoke ourselves to Him *through the kind of personhood we develop*. We can aspire to become like those of whom Paul wrote to Corinth: "You yourselves are our letter of recommendation, written on our hearts, to be known and read by all men, and you show that you are a letter from Christ . . ." *(2 Corinthians 3: 2,3)*.

Our Inner Attitudes

Despite all the attention that we may give to studying and to deepened intellect, the most stirring quality in devotion is *attitude*. Our attitudes are our belief-tendencies, our dispositions to act, our readiness pattern. Growing in the personhood of Jesus' values means an increasing readiness to affirm the Lord, to be open to Him. If we look to the declared mission of Jesus, we see a theme of attitude: Jesus stated that He was "... to preach good news to the poor ... to proclaim release to the captives and recovering of sight to the blind, to set at liberty those who are opressed, to proclaim the acceptable year of the Lord" *(Luke 4:18, 19).* To understand these tasks, devoted followers of Jesus find health and peace in maintaining a vigilance for *self-renewal.* The concerns of Jesus in this mission, if they become our own, are not self concerns. But we do need the strength of renewing ourselves in the personality of the Lord.

How to be a self-renewing person in living a life of devotion is soundly supported by four tactics. In responses to Christ the Giver, we are able to be receivers with greater openness *by taking inventory of ourselves, by changing through gaining new concepts, by turning crises into priveleges and by understanding how values guide choices.*

Personal Inventory

The first tactic, inventorying ourselves, is a sound prelude for almost any serious endeavor. We are accustomed to taking inventory of our equipment before beginning boating trips, hunting trips and most air flights. We know the value of checking strengths, proficiencies and weaknesses ahead of time. Spiritual stock-taking can also involve checking of strengths and weaknesses. To do this a person has access to many kinds of resources: study groups, prayer, the Bible and earnest inquiry with selected persons. "Who am I?"

This question, when asked spiritually, can become an almost-constant interest.

In many cases people hinder their devotional growth as a result of not determining their "hang-ups," those issues within their thinking that clash and create conflicts. Such a personal, interiorized conflict was held by the acclaimed Civil War general Thomas "Stonewall" Jackson.[13] Tanner describes the craving for distinction, for earthly, lasting fame expressed by General Jackson, who once confided to a staff member that he was afraid a certain battle during the Mexican War would not be severe enough to win him distinction. His craving for fame, however, clashed mightily with a genuine Christian humility. If we bend ourselves to serious devotion, we are probably able to uncover similar strains within ourselves. This kind of self-confrontation then offers a means for resolving the conflict.

New Images

Another valuable tactic in self-renewal is gaining new images. We are all image-builders for one another. My impressions of myself, for example, are greatly affected by your impressions of me as you convey them to me. This plain fact generates in many people a sense of responsibility for how they treat others. It is sobering to realize how much we influence the way other people feel about themselves. Peter Pan, we are told, failed to learn this lesson: he persisted in his pursuit of fantasy and fun without caring how he could change. As he failed to gain new images of himself, he was left behind by those whose maturing included new concepts of themselves.

The search for new images in Christian devotion is really a search for new meanings. The supervisor who fails to engage in labor relations talks with his own staff because he fears his tendencies to erupt in anger may be short-circuiting his own growth. The landlord who refuses to examine the unbearable housing conditions of his properties will hardly gain many new meanings or reflections of responsibility. Image-changing is simply the recognition that facts are perceptual: that what one can become rests upon new impressions and new hopes. If I can know a new image of *me*, then I can better come to know a new image of *you* and of my relatings to you.

From Crisis to Privilege

A third tactic in self-renewal, also perceptual in nature, is converting from attitudes of crisis to attitudes of privilege. This is the extraordinary process of prizing problems gratefully! Yes, this is the casting of a positive outlook *realistically*, to perceive problems as opportunities. It is possible to develop the habit of viewing routine chores, tough choices and distasteful assignments as being privileges. A self-renewer catches this image when he or she realizes that life itself is a problem. Take away the problems and see how vital life seems then!

The story is told of two little Indiana boys trudging through a field with their father, headed for a circus. The younger boy, perhasps 2½ years old, dropped a nickel he had been fondling. After a search in the grass, the small owner found it, only to hear his brother (age 4) say, "Dad, let me have a nickel—I want to lose one too!" The joy of coping with problems lies in the joy of seeking. The fun is in the going!

This tactic of deepening devotion in the self-renewer brings insight of how *the crisis of surviving* turns into *the privilege of living*. The average person probably never does any deep thinking until he gets in a hole. In living a life of devotion we can expect this insight to yield mending. Instead of feeling grievance, resentment or panic, we are more likely to grow in feeling gratitude. Managing oneself is the key to new management of our problems. As one man put it: "Don't resent growing old. A great many are denied the privilege."

Values and Choices

Understanding the place of value in a world of fact is a fourth tactic of the self-renewing person. As we understand how our purposes fashion our actions and choices, we learn to grasp the fact that our values hold the key. We can laugh at the story of the peasant who, being asked why he was lying across the railroad tracks, replied, "I'm going to commit suicide." When asked why he had beside him a loaf of bread, the peasant said, "In this country by the time a train gets here, a man could starve to death!" Even when indecisive, a man's values direct what he does.

Robert Frost has observed "how way leads on to way" in his stirring poem "The Road Not Taken." Like stepping-stones, values carry us toward outcomes. If we think evil, we tend to do or be evil. If we value dispute, we tend to provoke dispute. If we value self-concentration, we tend to focus upon ourselves. If we value tiny deceits, we end up with accumulated lies and fakery. The influence of lies is unlikely to be healthful. It is this sobering disclosure that the self-renewer will find strengthening in his desire for mending.

Renewal Through Christ

Personal development in living a life of devotion as a spiritual personality unfolds through self-renewal. In our commitment to Christ we may expect to improve our openness to Christ by learning to reach for new concepts, by developing the sense of privilege in all transactions, by taking stock of oneself and by understanding better and better what are our values. These are processes by which we become more receptive to God's laws and mercy, more open to Christ's theme of mission. These are *mending* processes.

By making these more dominant in how we function, we contribute to our own healing and to that of others. While burdensome predicaments will undoubtedly continue to occur, the Christian can expect by these processes to attain a real and joyful wholeness.

Those devoted more committedly in awareness of Christ draw strength from their childlike confidence in God, finding relief and restoration. We are talking not only about meeting God but also about increasing association with Him. With simple confession of our sin, surrender to Him and more reverent attention to organizing our whole life around His wholeness, we experience rebirth and renewal. "Let us then with confidence draw near to the throne of grace, that we may receive mercy and find grace to help in time of need" (Hebrews 4:16).

---

1. William Pepperell Montague, *Belief Unbound* (New Haven: Yale University Press, 1930), pp. 66-67.
2. William Hocking, *The Coming World Civilization* (New York: Harper & Bros., 1956), p. 186.
3. C. S. Lewis, *The Weight of Glory* (Grand Rapids: Eerdmans, 1965), p. 15.
4. Ibid., p. 15.
5. Ernest T. Gordon, *Through the Valley of the Kwai* (New York: Harper & Row, 1962), p. 214.
6. Harry Emerson Fosdick, *The Hope of the World* (New York: Harper & Bros., 1933)), pp. 39-48.
7. Henry Steele Commager, *The Empire of Reason* (Garden City, New York: Anchor Doubleday, 1977), pp. 162-64.
8. George Buttrick, *So We Believe So We Pray* (New York: Abingdon, 1950), p. 25.
9. Lamgdon Gilkey, *Shantung Compound* (New York: Harper & Row, 1966), p. 116.
10. Ibid, p. 234.
11. Buttrick, *So We Believe So We Pray*, p. 177.
12. Elton Trueblood, *The New Man For Our Time* (New York: Harper & Row, 1970), p. 79.
13. Robert G. Tanner, *Stonewall in the Valley* (Garden City, New York: Doubleday, 1976), p. 53.

3

Through Suffering

*But my agony has fed
You, a moment, holy light.*
—John Hall Wheelock

One of the most powerful obstacles in Christian faith and a source of universal brokenness is suffering. None of us has to be instructed in the prevalence of human misery. The gifts of intelligence have afforded the world untold measures of control and relief through medicine, technology, social sciences and physical sciences. On all occasions across this earth, battles have been waged and won against a variety of perils. And yet heartache reaches into most homes and most lives, either in physical, mental or economic plans.

Only a few of us are willing to say with the Psalmist, "It is good for me that I was afflicted, that I might learn thy statutes" (Psalm 119:71). Only a masochist bent on self-tortue might be jollied by the wretchedness to be found everywhere. To those charged more specifically with supplying comfort and relief and to those weighted with the agonies of living, comes scant sense of victory in knowing of the hundreds of thousands of others who are bearing comparable hurts. Some lightening of despair does come, however, from feeling and seeing the sense of sharing of one's pains expressed to us by others, as Trueblood has noted.[1] When one realizes that his individual suffering is shared in spirit by someone else, or by many collectively, the pain is likely to lessen.

It is perfectly clear that attitudes may govern not only physical healing but also the onset of a sense of relief. The Psalmist's attitude, cited above, is one signal of the individualized perspective by which the Christian may proceed with mending. Those who do not want to get well, even when scientific assessment sees nothing but favorable conditions, may not improve. Those who truly *desire* to recover often *do* recover. The attitudes of desire and determination often act as elements of motivation. Beyond these facts, however, rests the gnawing question for many of us in the depths of despair: *"Why?"* Why *my* pain, *my* tragedy? Where is this God of mercy of which Christians speak?"

Understanding Suffering

If we focus on those caught in mental or spiritual ache, we can be encouraged by the effects that people experience from *understanding suffering*. Psychospiritual and interpersonal distresses *do* yield to new insights of this universe and of God's power at work in it. Veils of real misunderstanding block the kind of vision by which mending can proceed.

The most common dilemma among all of us is that of our *expectations*. We are reared to expect mostly rose gardens. Our "reality" in many cultures is shaped from fantasies. Even while we disclaim such a concept, we look forward to life as predominantly pleasure and painless rewards. We don't mind constructing some of our "pains," as in competitive athletics, since our whole conception of the process includes the final glory of victory. Mankind has long fashioned grueling ordeals for its members, but generally these have been set in a context where victory is possible and agony more or less temporary. However, whenever the pains are not of our own design and offer little hope for diminishing, then we deepen depression and feel a brokenness beyond bearing.

Invalid expectations guide many of us to unrealistic and unhelpful notions of natural and divine law. For example, I might recoil in disgust or resentment from the death of my son as an accident victim on his bicycle. Why? Because I may have been assuming that an all-powerful God controls *all* events at all times, including the vision of automobile drivers, tire tread traction, weather and the actions of a child on a bicycle. My assumptive world leads me to estrangement and bitterness. "If God cannot control the natural universe," I may feel, "then just what is He in charge of? If He *is* in charge, then how can He allow this kind of thing to happen?" Or I may broaden my bitterness to include all sufferers: "How could God permit sufferers to go on suffering endlessly?"

Purifying Attitudes

Under these conditions the mending heart needs a remedy in understanding. While invalid ideas may not be replaced quite as neatly as is done in the installation of organ implants or of new car batteries, these notions need correction. How we come to understand, through Christ, needless suffering or tragedy requires both religious training and truths about the inexorable functioning of the physical world. Nels Ferre stated, "Religion can become real through suffering only as we learn to accept it."[2] As long as we reject suffering, we will be using denial irrationally. But the way in which we accept suffering offers a means for healing.

The torture of our expectation will lessen as we fit ourselves to the truth of this plant and its circumstances physically. God is *not* controlling all brakes; all disease germs; or the minds of all drivers, pilots and frenzied gunmen, any of which may dispense suffering in a moment. Christian faith for many, however, does allow for divine intervention in ways and at moments which resist explanation. Accidents, as transgressions of physical laws, and diseases do take place. What we accept as reality requires us to accept these facts and their consequences. Bones do break, engines do fail, minds do fail to function properly and body cells do become diseased when certain conditions are violated.

Generally the heart begins mending as we come to understand that the suffering in life is *natural*, that it is a natural outcome of physical existence. This simple though profound insight produces two ideas: 1) *suffering teaches*, and 2) *suffering strengthens*. We have the illumination of Ferre's account of his deep sense of injustice about his own affliction and the death of his baby daughter. He wrote:

> Why should I of all people have such a handicap? Of course, unfortunate things did happen in the world, but not to such as I, who wanted to spend their whole lives for God. . . . Yet it was not enough that my pain got worse; I had to watch helplessly as my baby daughter suffered

and died. It took that and more before I was willing to own that I needed very much to have my strong self-will broken; that my pride and efficiency were of no use to God until He could teach me concern in the community of suffering. No one ever comes to know God and experience love until he has suffered.[3]

The Lesson of Living

This lesson of living is hard to learn. Our rigid wills hold us back within the confines of a narrowed picture of the world and life and our place in it all. Just as an alcoholic can hardly rehabilitate until bottom is hit, so we the sufferers can hardly shatter our fears in resisting God's love until we experience the darkness of suffering. But with His grace we can feel the whole new vitalizing love by which we are taught the enlarging conception of life. This experience and this idea together represent the lesson of *mending through learning and loving*.

As the Christian's faith deepens its roots, like grass, it stretches upward in health. The rising of strength in the sufferer equates to stamina. In place of a tormented spirit, the Holy Spirit provides both courage and durability. We have this encouragement from Paul:

> If God is for us, who is against us? . . . Who shall separate us from the love of Christ? Shall tribulation, or distress, or persecution, or famine, or nakedness, or peril, or sword? As it is written, For thy sake we are being killed all the day

long. . . . No, in all these things we are more than conquerors through Him who loved us *(Romans 8:31, 35-37)*.

When we understand suffering to be weaker than our relation to Christ, *we look at and react to suffering differently*. Out of our Christian faith comes *His* strength.

Psychotherapists are aware of the hoplessness and helplessness found in many persons suffering depression. The abyss of despair is marked by feelings of futility. Nothing seems to work; no hope of relief is in sight; and we see ourselves locked in a situation without promise of help. Sometimes these conditions are real, but in other cases they are more perceptual than real. These are the times when the experience of being a conqueror seems absolutely impossible. It is then that expectation is dismal.

Understanding Myself

Another common dilemma of misunderstanding which increases fears and worsens reactions to suffering is *the understanding of self*. So many human beings possess a fragile sense of self that miseries quickly break their spirits. We often grow up using pretensions. We fantasize and deceive ourselves with false mental images. These false deceptions then become large weaknesses in our lives. We think we are much better, much prettier and much more unique than we actually are; or else we think ourselves much weaker, much more unattractive and much less distinguished than we actually are. Through whatever pattern of delusion that each of us may have, there may be the habit of rebelling against God, of seeking to be gods to ourselves. Even in the most earnest of Christ's followers these forms of deception and disobedience may be present.

Many persons live quite well for long periods of their lives without their misunderstood selves showing its vulnerability. This means that we roll along without the real self being tested. After all, society has not formed bureaus or government agencies for the purposes of auditing "selves." We have no "self-scanners" or x-ray-like equipment for checking the condition of self. For many persons, successes and commendations tend to underline the value of their selves. We are acclaimed for our conquests, personalities and advancement in secular programs. We even carry small crosses of burden or grief while marching forward with some of the inward deceptions and disobediences remaining obscured.

The Answer to Ignorance

Jesus spoke of ignorance and falsehoods (John 7:18; Matthew 15:8,9). You and I may easily remain ignorant of how we each contribute to distortions of self in others. We may be ignorant of how we subtract dignity from a person or of how we scar major impressions of his own self. While being vocal in our nominal affirmation of the Lord, we may respond more to the doctrines of contemporary, popular leaders and scholars. The precepts of men may shape our efforts more than the teachings of Jesus shape what we are. Meanwhile we may be edging toward our own brokenness as we bind ourselves so fully in the culture that we lose acuity in even distinguishing what is pagan from nonpagan.

From the Christian perspective the mending of the brokenhearted will require some rehabilitation of self-understanding. The mending heart is one in which illusions are hunted and dissolved. Hallowed private images of self will be uncovered and laid aside forever. In many of our predicaments you and I cannot mend or contend until we yield authentically to God.

Faith alive—this is the point! It is faith that lifts and renews the downhearted. C.S. Lewis put it plainly by saying, "Reason may win truths; without Faith she will retain them just so long as Satan pleases."[4]

Knowing Who We Are

Knowing who we really are is a large part of mending. Tissues of the soul constitute religious faith. As long as these tissues harbor rebellious notions or pride-distorted ingredients of self, we are likely to be deeply troubled, in despair or miserable. God is *the* Power, and our conception of ourselves must be brought into harmony with Him. The lessons of suffering impact on us in a way which lifts out our defiances and diminishes our delusions. Suffering is so sobering that truths spring out everywhere.

God's love not only reaches in with tenderness beyond description, but also removes the veils through which we look at things. We change through His love. We change what we are expecting; life no longer looks like a big bowl of jellybeans with our name on it. We change in our honesty of self; we want to put away the games, lay aside the sham and yeild to His comforting love. We want to clear accounts, to set fundamentals where we know they belong, to live simply in His care according to His will. And we *feel* His power as we have never before felt power. Affliction is a mighty teacher, sure to gain our attention, uniquely persuasive and instructive. We can begin mending as Christ lifts us to a new understanding of the real struggle we *should* be making as contrasted with the more self-oriented, rebellious and indignant struggle we have likely *been* making.

Ferre shares vividly how this letting go to God often prefaces the long-awaited relief we desire.[5] It is a feeling accompanied by acceptance of our plight. It is as if we stop fighting or resenting our plight by then receiving God's current of hope and inspiration. Many people offer testimony of this sequel.

We should by all means seek the best of medical, dental, psychological and spiritual counsel for combating our particular suffering. We may require professional insights from well-trained and sensitive practitioners, knowing that their expertise is simply another form of God's resources for healing. But we will do well to consider how a final, total yielding to God appears to serve as a threshold for entry into the health or strength by which various mending forces bring relief.

Conquering Through Christ

Another important perspective is the way hardships are conquerable through Christian faith and Christ. Hardships will likely continue in our lives, but they can be reperceived in this form: what happens to me is incidental—*what counts is how I can turn my circumstances to the glory of God and the sevice of others*. His glory—not mine!

This fundamental turnaround in attending to the present privilege to work for God's purposes, instead of dwelling on our dilemma, signals two important shifts—*from self-concern to God*, and *from the past to the present and future*. These are the shifts by which we gain real understanding of our sufferings. This is how we are led to new visions of purpose.

The eminent psychiatrist Viktor Frankl has shown the value of this breakthrough in understanding in many of his patients. Frankl told of the rabbi who had lost his first wife and six children at Asuchwitz. Because he was unable to have other children, the rabbi felt great despair in realizing that he could not expect, as a sinner, to gain entry to heaven or to have a son who would pray for him after death. As the rabbi was led to see that his own faith could lead to spiritual refinement by virtue of his long years of suffering, he saw new meaning in his own survival, and hence relief.[6]

Purpose Provides Therapy

If we can feel or find a certainty in our suffering, it is quite likely that we shall make this shift in attitude, a shift therapeutic in itself. Pointless, futile suffering indeed worsens our brokenness. But in reaching the bottom of such a valley of darkness, if we encounter a challenge or purpose in the meaning of our unavoidable misery, we are then ready to receive new images of value in our affliction or suffering.

A few years ago we had a male patient in his late fifties who was hard of hearing and suffered from glaucoma. He had dwindled in deep despair to the point that he rejectd surgery and refused all help. His Christian faith had sufficient substance to permit me to ask him one day, "You claim to care about children. If you were healthy again and back in your trade full time, would you take time to help boys learn your art of whittling?" This man, despite his sensory handicaps, was a skillful carver; yet he said nothing at that point. "I know a boy with no father who wants to learn whittling. If I brought him here, would you mind showing him how to do a few things properly?" He only nodded, but from that step he led himself gradually out of his deep resentment against his own unhappiness to bright, smiling classes with a boys' club. Several months later he said to me, "I know now what is worthwhile!" His recovery continued through people and achievements.

Losing Heart and Gaining Hope

In countless kinds of depression, especially where conditions offer no hope of change, the brokenhearted often lose heart. They lose the capacity to form new relationships with either persons or things. This relational isolation tends to breed unhappiness about unhappiness, greater captivity for the basic captivity. Finding one tendril of interest in such cases may allow for one feeble step toward relations, toward meaning. Without relations the human creature is without hope. And in hopelessness one loses the ability to reflect and see reflections. This is the desolation, the deadness into which Jesus may enter. Mending of heart resumes with the realization of some new significance—a drawing, a talk, a service performed, some glimpse of meaning which reestablishes a link with *explanation* or *new association*. Then suffering invariably softens.

Have you ever thought about how, when things stop making sense, you lose interest in them? If bowling has been important to you, and you finally discover one day how "senseless" it has become in your present way of life, you will feel your interest subside. If the church ceases to make much sense to you, the chances are that you will lose interest in it. So too, if your aches and unnecessary oppression appear senseless, your life soon stops making sense. Most of us need to feel some kind of explanation for our sufferings if we are to continue in wholeness of spirit.

The all-too-familiar cases of dropouts among the youth of America show this same symptom. Here are thousands of young persons who fail to find meaning in life and society. With their new freedoms to rebel, many young people reject the system and lose the sense of meaning which they need for striving. For many of them, despair is so abundant that they become very vulnerable to sin, confusion and degrading drug habits.

Meaning in Christ

The Christian faith, however, can provide a psychic and a spiritual base for rediscovering meaning. Suffering uniquely prepares a person for insight: "Oh, how I see *now* what I have not seen before!" It may take only a seemingly trivial event, one conversation, or one kind of contact with a place or person to bring a quick disclosure of truth. A new seminary student, age 34, reports his disclosure occuring while on an extended cross-country hike, where he became a different *interpreter*. His experiences, while largely alone, included just enough "miracle" gifts and provisions that his attention drew him straight to Providence and new purposes. Although we may need the help of others at times in sorting things out, we are sure that ordeals bring clarity.

Clairty of outlook stems from clarity of insight that we too have a cross to be shouldered. Christian conviction is fortifying; we no longer need to resent or deny disaster; we shed our illusions of the easy routes through life. Instead, we build a fortress in our inner lives within which we cope with sin, injustice and stress as they offer themselves to us.[7]

Answers to Our Torments

When we stumble and falter under obsession with our torments, we often dwell upon 1) the inequities we see, and 2) the technology and economics so abundantly cruicial in all that surrounds us. Our image of man as god becomes blurred; we become doubtful as we agonize over the apparent inadequacy of this world to solve our helplessness. We feel lost; for man locked in despair is lost from himself and God. In this day of our lives, John Nef suggests, "We must find man again, and the way to do that is not to seek first *his* dignity. It is to seek first the dignity that God has confided to him."[8]

Sufferings can reorient us to a God-powered world. His resource, if given priority in all that we are thinking, becomes our new power. God discloses again the dignity we have so often overlaid with a combination of vanity and pride. God teaches once more how we are to feel and what we are to see. God sends people to us to demonstrate His love. God illuminates our options in this free world, options that we have been overlooking in our gloom and wrong assumptions.

Sufferings lead us away from the body and mind as the prime leaders in our existence. We instead start our mending again by following our soul. Out in the bright daylight our soul becomes far more real than it has been previously. God reveals Himself to our soul, and we must familiarize ourselves with the soul if it is to gain primacy in guiding us to the restoration we prize. This means that our spiritual growth can no longer be taken for granted. Nor can it be ignored. Our Christian faith, developing in our soul, can remove the pain and soothe us in the deepest of calamity. But our soul must be known and verified as realistically as our body or reasoning processes. "Soul" must become more than some abstract theological concept—it must become *experience*.

Knowing the Love of God

This experiencing of one's soul is what permits a person to move toward a more perfect love of God. Feeling love for God becomes an event of soul, a reciprocal for His love to stream into us in our predicaments. "For God is at work in you, both to will and to work for his good pleasure" *(Philippians 2:13)*. Feeling not alien from Him, but closely attended by Him, is the means for knowing His comforting love.

The dignity of a person *as person* can be rediscovered only through this experience of connection with God. William Barclay, the renowned and perceptive Scottish preacher, has written a searchingly simple "testament of faith" entitled *A Spiritual Autobiography*. He expresses his belief in Jesus by citing a portion of a John Drinkwater poem which refers to Shakespeare, Shelley and Socrates. This is what he said: These "others we know about; Jesus we know. The others we remember: Jesus we experience. . . . I find it very difficult to distinguish between the Holy Spirit and the ever-present Risen Lord. It is the coming of the Spirit which is to take away the desolation of the disciples. . . . It is the Spirit who is to convict man of his own sin and of Jesus' righteousness. . . . It is the Spirit who is to bring the new truth, as men are able and ready to receive it. . . ."[9]

Barclay expresses his feeling that Paul believed the same way, as Paul said: "Now the Lord is the Spirit. . . " *(Corinthians 3:17)*. Barclay feels satisfied that the Spirit and the Risen Lord are one in action. He alludes to the concept of G.H.C. Macgregor, that the Holy Spirit is Jesus Christ's *alter ego*. Knowing Jesus directly in experience is how a person uncovers the dignity God has confided in him—whether on bended knee or in heavy heart. The new truth is a truth of the soul.

God's Communications

The new truths (or the old truths rediscovered), that come to us in our soul through Christian faith and ordeals, are God's communications to us. Oh, how the heavyhearted need communications! Oh, how they need the comfort of God's mind! Oh, how they need the purity of thought freed from the static of self! It is almost as if we cannot be receivers until we are bowed beneath our ordeals. Is it that we cannot inherit until we are meek?

The solace of the Christian sufferer lies in Jesus. Here is the source of assurance that God grieves when we bear grief, that He is tormented when we are in torment. Here is the comfort from which mending tissues commence their renewal. For those choking in the ferment of their bitterness, the meaning of suffering is kept from bringing solace. Yet the strong, quiet awakening power of Christian faith can pierce even the most impenetrable walls of despair. "He heals the brokenhearted, and binds up their wounds" *(Psalm 147:3)*. "Thou wouldest not seek Me," says Pascal, "if thou didst not possess Me. Be not therefore troubled."[10]

As Christians consider the meaning of God's patterns and sequences in the Good News, they dwell upon His designation of certain types and conditions of humble behavior to which God draws man's attention:

> I thank thee, Father, Lord of heaven and earth, that thou has hidden these things from the wise and understanding and revealed them to babes; yea, Father, for

> such was thy gracious will. . . . Come to me, all who labor and are heavy-laden, and I will give you rest. Take my yoke upon you, and learn from me; for I am gentle and lowly in heart, and you will find rest for your souls. For my yoke is easy, and my burden is light *(Matthew 11:25-30).*

Jesus was uttering thanks to the Father for providing *insights* to those troubled and humble. The Good News could be received by those bearing heavy burdens. For those facing ridicule or feelings of unworthiness, the Good News and the yoke of Christ were offered as confidence. The scoffers offer scorn and conditions are oppressive, the lowly in heart find the rest they need in the Lord. When we feel as if nothing matters (most of all ourselves), the message of Christianity comes through that we *do* matter to God.

The Blockage of Pride

The world two thousand years ago and the world today necessarily emphasize the link between pride and the inability to receive Christ's message. In man's nature is the possibility of becoming separated from God through the self-glorification which accompanies education and secular world privileges. In gaining wisdom of this world, power and material possessions, we run the risk of becoming insensible to the meaning of lowliness and the humbling signified by God through Jesus. There is nothing wrong with learning facts of this world and acquiring skills for performing credibly in the world—only in the consequences of such training as they lift us into pride. There is nothing wrong with prosperity—only in the arrogance or deafness it so easily invokes. "But the cares of the world, and the delight in riches, and the desire for other things, enter in and choke the word, and it proves unfruitful" (Mark 4:19). Human creatures are remarkably self-delusive; whenever they are filled with power or luxurious privilege, they tend to worship self alone. Yet the inevitable disasters and disappointments to be encountered in the world can restore both hearing and humility in a hurry!

In Pascal's words, "Misery induces despair, pride induces presumption. The Incarnation shows man the greatness of his misery by the greatness of the remedy which he required."[11] In the words of a Peter Marshall prayer, ". . . We are too Christian really to enjoy sinning and too fond of sinning really to enjoy Christianity. Most of us know perfectly well what we ought to do; our trouble is that we do not want to do it. Thy help is our only hope. . . ."[12] God's help indeed comes to us in the lowliness of our suffering—what we need to be made whole and to feel relief.

Questions and Answers

In closing this chapter on mending through suffering, we must pause to examine briefly the apparent satisfaction of a whole life for those who either deny God or worship other gods. Some Christians feel doubt as they observe the long life of health and happiness enjoyed by such persons. "How do non-Christians bear their hardships at times without the restorative effects of Christian faithfulness?" "If faith and deep devotion to Christ represent victory over brokenness for a Christian, how does the atheist fare so well?"

Two observations need to be made. First, we are given freedom to make choices, to select conclusions from which to go forward toward understanding. Second, we are to meet circumstances for which our limitations restrict our understanding. The Christian is a creature who *believes first*, as a prelude to understanding. In Barclay's declaration of his own belief, he borrows the perspective of Anselm: "I do not seek to understand so that I may believe; rather do I believe that I may understand."[13] As the Christian begins with acceptance, faith produces experiences through which understanding unfolds. But not all situations in life will be "understood" or explained through faith. We shall not find all answers just as we shall not find all power within our grasp. We shall not perceive what transpires within all persons, nor shall we discern the actual experiences of atheists.

Begin With Faith

What the Christians can do, however, is to begin with faith and go straight on through sufferings meaninglessness and defeat with that conviction which yields to the experience of God's attitude, love and presence. The Christian can behave in response to the Word of God. The Christian begins and proceeds from this posture of affirmation. God is the Master of this universe, the Creator of spiritual beings, the Originator of love. The Christian begins with and receives in experience the revelations of God. We can be sure that suffering teaches and that it fortifies—not through chance, but through the presence of Jesus Christ. We dare to speak as believers with the Psalmist: "Gracious is the Lord, and righteous; our God is merciful. The Lord preserves the simple; when I was brought low, he saved me. . . . For thou has delivered my soul from death, my eyes from tears, my feet from stumbling. . . " *(Psalm 116:5-8).*

---

1. Trueblood, *The Life We Prize*, p. 187.
2. Nels Ferre, *Making Religion Real* (New York: Harper & Bros., 1955), p. 143.
3. Ibid., p. 143
4. C.S. Lewis, *Christian Reflections* (Grand Rapids: Eerdmans, 1971), p. 43.
5. Ferre, *Making Religion Real*, p. 144.
6. Viktor Frankl, *Man's Search For Meaning* (New York: Simon & Schuster, 1959), pp. 119-20.
7. John U. Nef, *Cultural Foundations of Industrial Civilization* (New York: Harper & Row Torchbook, 1960), p. 96.
8. Ibid., p. 155.
9. William Barclay, *A Spiritual Autobiography* (Grand Rapids: Eerdmans, 1975), p. 109.
10. Blaise Pascal, *Pascal's Penses* (New York: Dutton, 1958), No. 554.
11. *Pensees*, No. 525.
12. Peter Marshall, *Mr. Jones, Meet the Master* (New York: Revell, 1949), p. 145.
13. Barclay, *A Spiritual Autobiography*, p. 36.

4

Through Service

*How by being miserable for myself I began,
And now am miserable for the mass of man.*
—George Barker

The secret is simple: when I lend you my shoulder or tend to your aches, my own weakness is reduced! If I focus *where you are* and reach out to you, then I can hardly hold my gaze on myself and my own plight. The real beauty in God's loving patterns of creation includes this fact.

This principle conforms to physiology: exercise produces vigor, taxing of tissues produces strength. For surgical patients today there is a general practice of seeking very early return to their feet. Indulgence of tissues has been found to be debilitating. *Putting tissues to work again is part of therapy.*

My own mending of spirit follows this principle. As I find a way to use my faith in behalf of someone else, I take a step toward wholeness. On the other hand, my emotional prosperity may dissipate if my faith is left inert and makes concern for myself predominant. As long as I dwell only on my own predicamnt, I will likely generate more circles of confusion and depression. But if I turn to create relief for *you*, my own sense of anguish begins to lighten.

Christian Faith at Work

Let us see what the Christian faith at work in fellowship looks like. In the first place, it is *inclusive*. Christians will include themselves in *your* suffering; they will include the estranged. In the memoirs of Lev Kopelev we learn of such an inclusion as he recounts an incident of Easter Sunday. Kopelev, one of the most passionate scholars in the civil rights movement in the USSR, had been confined in prison for alleged anti-Soviet activities. He tells how one day in April one of his fellow-inmates, Aunt Dusya, invited several people to a secret observance of Easter, to be held in one of the women's barracks which had been made into an improvised chapel. "So what if you are unbelievers?" Aunt Dusya said. "You and Seryozha stand up for people, and whoever stands up for people stands up for God. . . . You and Seryozha, and your Edith, you are people with soul. I see right into you, and what I see is good, and I pray for you as for one of my own."[1]

Kopelev goes on to describe the plea made by Aunt Dusya for inviting the informer, Stepan. She argued that Stepan's poor, dark, lost, sinful soul might make difficult his finding a ray of light in prison. "Let him see that even here, in prison," went the argument of Aunt Dusya, "the light of Christ still shines and there is pity even for such as he."

The long-excluded lepers in the early days of Christianity provided an example of how God's attitudes toward men were to signify outreach and inclusion, even to the most reprehensible. Here is simply the *attitude of service*—"*you* come first in what you *are* rather than in what you *look like* or what you have *just said* or what you have *done.*" How more eloquently could the Lord have expressed this attitude than in his footwashing love of His disciples?

Limited Outlooks

Human Creatures get encapsulated in their own filaments of outlook. Let me put this another way: we tend to remain locked within our own perceptual worlds until or unless we acquire exploratory skills for discerning new relations and alternatives. We are not able to visualize new possibilities. Without a deepening sense of enrichment, we stifle at times in our own limiting outlook. We lack the freshness of perspective in valuing ourselves that is basic if we are to amplify our projection in faith. We need a morsel to taste, a sample to feel, if we are to amplify our capacities to God; at least most of us do.

This conception of what human beings need to break out of their self-spawned isolation (and it may often be desolation) is supported by the work of one of the most provocative scientists involved in educational theory, Jerome Bruner. In his exciting little book *Toward A Theory Of Instruction*, he says that "discovering how to make something comprehensible to the young is only a continuation of making something comprehensible to ourselves in the first place—that understanding and *aiding* others to understand are both of a piece."[2] Bruner had been struck by the importance of training individuals in subtle spatial imagery by exposing them to fresh experiences in visualizing their surroundings. To those lost in hopelessness, there must come other people who demonstrate examples of hope. These others can aid in restoring hope by simply expressing the nature of their own comprehensions of faith. We all know something about memorizing, for example, but we may be relatively unexposed to the varied experiences of "faithing."

Affirming True Faith

What I am suggesting is the possibility that Christians in serving others may be presenting examples of how to faith—how to feel, how to know and how to affirm the God of Christians. Elton Trueblood notes the cruciality of our knowing both God and our own wretchedness, from which God the Redeemer can bring freedom.[3] Christian faith necessarily is a process of *experiencing*, and with God's grace and the presentation of faith in serving others, we who are broken may begin to increase our response to God, to increase our spiritual power, and to overcome our hopelessness.

When others come in selfless service to me, I can hardly evade the clear message that I matter to them. For a little while at least, I am meaningful—not meaningless. For most humans around this earth this message penetrates. "I'm *included*," goes my thinking: "they wish to share themselves with me and to show their concern for my load!" There is no question that those who receive the warmth and relief brought by others feel a new strength. But what of those *who are bringing* this warmth and relief? Who learns more—the teacher or the pupil?

If I am to be comprehensible in what I carry as a servant to someone else in need, I can only do so by extending from my own comprehension. My effects will be little different from my own clarity and integrity.

Be Helped by Helping

It is plain that we *begin or continue our own mending as we prepare for mending for others*. When I go out to serve another person, some parts of me get transformed. And while I am enroute and involved in direct serving, I am further transformed. These are changes of the soul and mind together. They may be unconscious. They may be latent, not surfacing where I or others notice them as changes for hours, days or weeks, but they are real. If I go to serve in His name, in my Christian faith I have the assurance that Jesus will gather there too, bringing the strength of His presence. "Where two or three are gathered in my name, there am I in the midst of them" *(Matthew 18:20)*.

These inner preparations for mending call attention to a second attribute of those who would counsel and aid recuperation: their *tender patience*. To be effective as a servant requires enduring patience. So, many times those who are troubled or who are in trouble are not ready to admit they need help. If you are sick and despairing, you might be more than ready for an offer of assistance. But in many instances we have an ego problem. We cannot admit we are at our bottom; we are not ready to surrender. The alcoholic is likely to suffer this barrier for too long a time. Once the ego gets shrunk and our pride ebbs, then we may be primed to talk with someone, hopefully a person with tender and patient understanding. Occasionally the pathological liar or the compulsive gambler will have faced such shocking damages resulting from his conduct that he too will welcome a chance to make a new psychospiritual start. But whatever the burden, sufferers frequently respond to tenderness.

In the Alcoholics Anonymous (AA) program we observe the mending processes: those with greater health help those with lesser health. One part of the success in AA is believed to be the *sensitivity* which operates in the relationship between the discloser and the listener. John Keller tells us how disclosure of wrongs is part of the whole recovery process instigated through AA.[4] When patience and understanding preside, an alcoholic can lay open two important facts: 1) the exact nature of his hurts and wrongs, and 2) the pride buried more deeply than all his other misdeeds. When this disclosure is made to God, then the real spiritual journey begins. "Journey deep within thy self, and listen by the way."

The Christian who serves another person finds new openness with himself. It is difficult to be tender toward others without becoming tender inside, to be receptive toward others without becoming receptive toward self. Uncovering blockages in oneself while ministering to someone else with blockages is quite a rich dividend.

Coming Home to Reality

There comes into play while serving others not only more tenderness but also greater authenticity. As my pride grows smaller, I feel as if I have come home to myself. At least the route home is more clear. Just hearing the disclosures flow out of the depths of a person in great torment seems to clear away the fog of one's own murky depths. "When I was traveling home from Haiti, where I labored building a dining room and a chapel with fellow Christians," reported a man recently, "I saw much more clearly some of my own elements of spiritual ineffectiveness." Service works a beautifully gentle scouring effect upon the servant. This may be another version of Bruner's "exposure" concept—the benefits incurred from exposure to new dimensions of old surroundings.

It is hard to spell out in specific terms what this reciprocal effect entails, but we are sure that a person profits in providing what he most needs himself for mending. "Blessed are those who give." In the nature of giving to someone else what they need (and what I need as well), I shall very likely *receive*. It is as if in order for me to serve another person in stress, I must first pass through their improbable dream world to reach reality in my own, not unlike Lewis Carrols' "Alice in the Looking Glass" world.[5] Like a strong whiff of ammonia, service clears the passages and wakes us up.

Sacrifice at Work

A third attribute of Christian faith at work in fellowship is *sacrifice*. Those who seek a healing of heart may well find therapy in making outright gifts of time, energy, convenience and self to someone else in deep stress. Who was the greater gainer—the wretch by the side of the road or the compassionate Samaritan whose mercy was rendered inconveniently? Many people, both Christians and non-Chrisitnas, know well this story of the event on the road to Jericho, but how often and deeply does it persuade new performances? We are too much like Moliere's character, Alceste, in *The Misanthrope*, who said:

> Can I thus triumph over all my love? ...
> Have I a heart that's ready to obey? ...
> But that's not all my weakness, I'm afraid;
> You'll see me carry it to exaggeration,
> And show how far from reasonable men are,
> For man's essential frailty hides in the heart.[6]

We take, and we receive; we absorb, covet and ingest. We learn (and earn rewards at times) to serve ouselves. The occasions of sacrifice become taboo for us. We don't wish to have the risks or the inconveniences attached to the sacrifice of plans. With such selfishness we can hardly grasp the concept that we are denying ourselves a healing agent. "What!" we exclaim. "Give up an hour, give up a day? It just can't be done." The renouncing of pleasure in order to serve someone else is often considered absurd. Yet in Christian faith it is the *servant* who gains from whatever service demands.

How easy it is to miss the therapeutic point in Jesus' response to the question, "Lord, when did we see thee hungry or thirsty or a stranger or naked or sick or in prison, and did not minister to thee?" "Truly, I say to you, as you did it not to one of the least of these, you did it not to me" (*Matthew 25:44, 45*).

This therapeutic opportunity abounds almost as much in the office, the store or the home as it does "on the road to Jericho." It is an opportunity for *attitude and action*. For us to mend we must in Christian faith carry *the tendency to care* and *the habit of follow-through*. It is easy to aspire, more difficult to deliver.

Our Inner Adversaries

Our old familiar culprits, pride and self, link up with fatigue and indifference to comprise a rugged adversary. We are proud; we are selfish; we are tired; and there are so many diversions that we feel compelled to shrug off "sacrificing" just to keep our balance most of the time. As we plod along with these influences predominating, we strangely encounter defeats or injuries so massive that we develop brokenness. It is then that we may discover the dividends inherent in becoming a servant to someone else.

What are we like as we feed and tend Christ's sheep? We draw circles which include them with us, we open ourselves in tender mercy to their needs, we give up something of ourselves in being helpful to them in their plight. How are we to understand that our wholeness begins its return through caring about and caring for another person? Part of the understanding lies in our changing of models, and part of it lies in shifting priority from ourselves.

A person's brokenness, even when it involves physical affliction, represents a stunted, unrealistic self. A human being is made stunted by deficits if impressions. When we center upon self for homogenized impressions, we deny our nature with God, and we are ill-equipped to handle the vigorous, threatening factors which roll across our path. To be *self-contained* is a form of arrested development. To prosper in the fullest sense, we need an infusion of models, of concepts, of this life, of the environment and of our spiritual place in all of these. Most of all, we need a bona fide model of love by which to organize our purpose and our energies.

Distortions of Self

Some examples might help to clarify the importance of changing models. If we consider one extreme of deviancy, the violent and long-term robber, we can probably see that he or she very likely bears a distorted concept of both self and love, of both self and society, of both self and God. If we look at the throbbing pains of marital discord, we find similar distortions of self in the relations of two persons to each other, other people in their acquaintanceship or to God. Models mean the shape of one's impressions: the constructions of the mind and heart by which the inner world guides reactions. Mending the heart regularly demands some changing of these constructions, not the least of which is the spiritual mode.

This condition of a person broken in spirit must not be regarded defensively, but it is important to identify properly that the *self is hindered and poorly developed*. When we are caught despondently within our injuries, darknesses or defeats, our selves may need a new benchmark. In Christian faith, God through Jesus provides this reference point by which to determine and generate new images of possibility.

Sometimes it is not easy to help a troubled person shift attention from self. We are great imitators and copiers. We match our conduct, as we grow up, to what we observe others doing—their values, their words, their fads, their thoughts and their interests. We watch how others speak, and we copy them. This is why it is easy for most of us to dwell upon ourselves: we see so many others doing it.

Another striking challenge in being mended is the problem of keeping others out, of resisting overtures of help. The sufferer in torment may not be ready (or not appear ready) to be "healed" or helped. On several occasions we find Jesus in the Bible asking, "Do you want to be healed?" (See for example, John 5:6.) The Holy Spirit works and reaches us through *people* to awaken our desire for wholeness. One of the most effective means for diminishing self-obsession is love. As Blake said, "He who will not bend to Love must be subdued by Fear." Those who serve others while needing relief themselves convey some of this fear-shattering love that aids others to shift their priority of attention. In helping someone else to new predispositions and a new desire to mend, I am charging up my own new predispositions.

Three Secrets for Mending

There are three aspects of building predispositions through service. They can be described in these three terms: *becoming active, clarifying through contrast* and *getting away from self*. Put another way, these mean that we mentally and spiritually get up and get going, that we see better by seeing into the patterns of others' experiences, and that we leave behind our self while doing it all.

Several conditions can trigger activation into service. One is sheer frustration, another is invitation and another is opportunity. If I am not frustrated by my personal strife, then I may feel little impulse to serve anyone else. But if my frustration is enormous, I may leap at the chance to console or assist someone else. We don't always see where or how we can offer assistance; or, if we do see, we may feel hesitancy. Here is where invitations, through God's grace and the Spirit, move opportunities in front of us. "Come join me," may go the invitation, or "Let's go visit." "Have you ever thought of helping the Grey Ladies group serve at the hospital?" Institutions, groups and organizations often possess missionary opportunities very near at hand for most persons.

Clarifying of oneself, once service is being pursued, involves experiencing. In relating to others in misery or brokenness, we experience many new perceptions, many new reflections on our own dilemma. This is really basic learning. "Would you drive Mrs. Huggins to her appointment at the hospital each week for six more weeks? She has no one to take her, and she never feels well after her treatments." You learn things you *need* to learn about yourself as you learn more about others. While your pains may not abate, you will likely hurt less; while your dilemma remains, you will feel relief from sharing yourself in the life of another. Who could deny that this kind of human event is a form of what Jesus meant by Christian fellowship at work?

Getting away from yourself is accomplished by pursuing a purpose other than yourself. If your service ventures have continuity (if your service to the Mrs. Huggins of your life gets expanded or extended), then your self-burden may be shelved. You are less able to fixate your own wound as you minister to someone else. In getting away from self, your service must be authentic; it must be honest and real.

From Self to Others

The self-understanding produced by acquiring new models and by shifting priority from self to others can often be a long process. God seems to permit this kind of revelation gradually, so that we don't buckle under the weight of seeing all of ourselves at once. Talking with someone about the personal journey on which we have started may be appropriate, especially as we reach a point where we want closer religious affiliaton. Getting more involved in selected readings may also be beneficial at the right point—not just any Christian books, but carefully chosen fiction and nonfiction. Somewhere along the line while talking, listening, reading or praying, conviction of new companionship will come, and the Living Lord will be sensed and treasured. From then on the length of the journey will not matter.

Your self-consciousness may not vanish; your answers won't all be yes or no; you won't necessarily know much of what is coming next; and your burden may still remain. But now you feel an unmistakable wholeness in His love. You feel better conditioned to go on, not only with your spiritual journey but also with your load.

With the love of God as our new connection in faith we rediscover the power and means of prayer. This coming into authenticity through God leads to a new candor regarding our sins and our redemption through the Lord. The harness of service is not tight; His yoke is easy, and our loads do lighten. As praying persons we gain new concerns, new sensitivity. We feel more responsible by feeling greater responsiveness. "Once open to the light, man may ask God to claim him more essentially and more profoundly. But on one condition only, on condition that he does not refuse the first small act that God demands of him."[7]

Redemption and Forgiveness

What is redemption, and what does it really have to do with mending of myself? It has everything to do with health and wholeness. It is forgiveness. It is God's special gift to us who come out from behind our masks to face our transgressions in His world. Oh, how often we scratch and cower in our dilemmas while abstaining from confession to Him, our Master! The unrealities we clutch are the barriers to our recovery. With them in position, how are we to overcome our separation from Him?

In serving we stand a chance, His chance, of becoming more authentic piece by piece. In serving we find it easy to give. All that we can give, God will take. And all that we are, He will take that too. When we are captured in endless anguish, we are likely to be lost. Finding out who we are is part of our movement toward health and relief, and also toward acknowledging that we belong to Him. In affirming that we are His, we make His demands more dominant, relinquishing our will to His.

In this light redemption is both a redeeming means and a redeeming end. It is a process of mending. Redeeming as a process leads us into *serving*. It takes us to the Jesus in others whatever their condition. And it is at the same time the *goal*, for it is in others and our bearing of His love to them that we come to find Him. Christian therapists know this truth. There is no recovery without His presence, whether those present at the time know it or not. He alone converts, forgives and heals.

Can't we save the chores, the tough things, till last? In a world of love, can we not press toward pleasures, feats and worldly treats, and have them first? What does a little larceny, a little corruption, a little fun hurt if I promise to straighten up at the end? So goes the query and often the pattern. But in Christian faith we see, even from within our tribulations, that Jesus turns this order around. The Cross precedes the Crown. We are consoled after we grieve. Happiness comes after the unhappiness.

Warped Cultural Values

We must admit that our culture teaches values that complicate our learning of Christian facts. For example, in most homes and communities pain is punishment. The way to respond to problems, defeats and disappointments is to emotionalize and even to cry or to retaliate. To a large degree, we are conditioned to magnify our hurts. Furthermore, we see held up as prizes the privilege of escape from menial functions. We are products of a forge shaping us to the consolation of luxuries of many kinds.

We can observe the benefits of agencies like the United Fund, in which communities band together in providing human service programs. And we can observe the value of the Red Cross, Big Brother and many church or religious organizations for treating the troubled in society. For the most part, however, these values remain secondary and peripheral to the central value of gaining victories through personal power. The ultimate we think, is to purchase whatever we desire—not to serve first God and then others. This is our *career-work ethic*.

Bruce Catton, exciting author of the Civil War series, once referred to the Southern troops describing the heavy battle at Sharpsburg as "artillery hell."[8] Most of us know how heavy the bombardment of our lives with defeats can be. We are cannonaded from all sides by fragmenting obstacles. There are times when we feel as if we are looking out upon a battlefield of demolished dreams. Our hearts become heavy and broken. Yet right where we are is God. Right where we are is an opportunity to tend to another. Right where we are we need to *put in first rank the practice of serving*, if we are to gain the wholeness we ultimately cry for.

True Trust in God

The mending heart is able to follow the path of service by trusting God. Larry Christenson offers encouragement in his delightful book *The Renewed Mind* as he points us to *thinking* God's thoughts, *feeling* God's emotion, *desiring* God's plan, *speaking* God's Word, and then *doing* God's work.[9] Here is the means for countering the career-work ethic that prevails within our culture and dominates so much of our thinking. Through prayer and service relationships we put these behavioral functions to work. We also have the word of Jesus, if we act upon it: "He who is one of God hears the words of God" (John 8:47).

Service as an attitude, as a preface to action, comes in the heart. The Christian faith is a product of God's Word being heard in the heart. "It is the heart which experiences God," says Pascal, " and not the reason. This, then, is faith: God felt by the heart, not by the reason."[10] Christian faith, by the testimony of Jesus, directs us to go in service with love to care for others.

I must turn also to the therapeutic truth we find stated in the words of Paul. Our *belief* is essential!

> The word is near you, on your lips and in your heart (that is, the word of faith which we preach); because, if you confess with your lips that Jesus is Lord and believe in your heart that God raised him from the dead, you will be saved *(Romans 10:8, 9).*

It is not enough to call upon the name of the Lord without belief in Him. The point is clear enough: we are to believe. Psychologically, whenever we act with lukewarm faith in any subject, we give only lukewarm acts. I will be a tepid performer in crossing a tightrope: if I have only tepid belief in its strength or in my own skills to walk across that wire. Whenever we go as Christians to serve, we are spiritually of God; and we must trust *Him*, listening for *His* words. As we then experience Him in our hearts, we are lending ourselves to His healing. Our responsibility is to be *of* God and open to Him. Nothing is better for the mind than to activate serving others by first serving God in our own hearts. It is there that we meet Him and experience His will for us to follow. Our believing becomes part of our mending; our faith can make us whole.

---

1. Lev Kopelev (trans. Anthony Austin), *To Be Preserved Forever* (Philadelphia: Lippincott, 1977), pp. 154-55.
2. Jerome Bruner, *Toward A Theory of Instruction* (Cambridge, Masswachusetts: Belknap Press, 1966), p. 38.
3. Elton Trueblood, *A Place to Stand* (New York: Harper & Row, 1969), p. 81.
4. John Keller, *Ministering to Alcoholics* (Minneapolis: Augsburg, 1966), p. 2.
5. Lewis Carroll, *Alice in Wonderland* (New York: Washington Square Press, Simon & Schuster, 1951).
6. Morris Bishop, trans., *Eight Plays of Moliers (The Misanthrope)* (New York: Modern Library, 1957), p. 282.
7. Adrienne von Speyr, (trans. Alexander Dru), *The Word* (London: Collins, 1953), p. 9.
8. Bruce Catton, "Mr. Lincoln's Army" from *The Army of the Potomac* (Garden City, New York: Doubleday, 1951), p. 293.
9. Larry Christenson, *The Renewed Mind* (Minneapolis: Bethany Fellowship Press, 1974), p. 133.
10. *Penses*, No. 278.

5

Through Love And Joy

For while in Him confiding
I cannot but rejoice
—William Cowper

To go forth in service when I myself am hurting seems as contradictory as finding happiness by being happy in the midst of unhappiness. "How can I experience love under such painful, unloving circumstances?" says the person snared in agony. We know that mankind through the centuries has wrestled with the burden of being joyless until hopes have been fulfilled. A human being cannot just be happy by willing it. Only after unsteady conditions have been stabilized in our favor can we really experience joy. The absoluteness of this relationship acts as a further bar to mending even though it is wholly false. The truth is that we *can* feel joyful, we *can* rejoice right in the midst of feeling pain or defeat! However, as long as we think we cannot do so, we will be hindered in regaining a sense of health.

It is so important to understand how we lose our sensibility when we glut our senses in the trough of despair. Sometimes we are compelled to react with pain when painful conditions are heaped upon us, to react with discouragement when all victory is taken away, to feel miserable when misery descends and persists. How are we to see, hear or sense the good, pleasant or the joyful when we are immersed in total wretchedness?

The Power of Faith

Christian faith provides the most durable power for this dilemma. God in His power through Jesus can touch the most deprived, most wretched of our moments. The human mind in its saddest moments can be penetrated by God's love.

Let me now turn to a few of these saddest moments. All of us have had some experience with pointlessness and heartrending anguish coming together to engulf us in despair. The Christian family must live with the torment suffered by their teenage son snared in drug abuse and horrible confusions. Despite this family's commitment in Christian faith and continuing vigil to the teachings of Jesus, the sad state of existence goes on. Where is the penetrating love of God for them?

Ordinarily most people can bear a little pain for at least a little while. But what of the 40-year-old son who must continue ministering to his 62-year-old father who is in constant deep pain, depleted of energy and hope for living? As this son prays and believes, in accord with his Christian faith that "your prayers will be answered," how is he to find God's love? Or what of the man who said a few years ago, "The good Samaritan was not attacked by the person he befriended. But my brother, as fine a Christian person as I have ever known, was hacked to death by some kind of motorist he had stopped to aid during a storm—where was God then?"

The idea of healing the self in such despair through love and joy can be almost unbearable or ludicrous. The bad in life can be so abundant that the human mind becomes buried in the weight of misery. Attitudes for focusing on joy seem lifeless. When all the avenues to pleasure are being demolished, isn't it a bit nonsensical to speak seriously of joy? How can one even think of love when standing so near to the anguish of the most unloving of life's conditions? Is this the dilemma expressed by the prophet? "O Lord, how long shall I cry for help, and thou wilt not hear? Or cry to thee 'Violence!' and thou wilt not save me? Why does thou make me see wrongs and look upon trouble?" *(Habakkuk 1:2,3)*.

New Attitudes Through Faith

The Christian in such a dilemma possesses potentials of attitudes by which Christian faith restores wholeness. One attitude in Christ which is restorative is the antidote to estrangement from understanding. In going into despair over misery, a person psychologically suffers from pointlessness. One's conceptions of life and living have been more or less based upon illusions, narrowed sentiments and self-deluding masks. One's understanding of life and self is precariously balanced upon a socialized role of privilege without much pain or defeat. In the words of Santayana, ". . . we wrap ourselves gracefully in the mantle of our inalienable part."[1] But when one's misery becomes far more than temporary, then a state of alienation is often begun. One cannot see the point, and one's understanding becomes inadequate. Estrangement in these terms is part of brokenhearted torment.

In a Christian, however, Christian faith offers an

antidote to estrangement. God's love does come, just as the seeker requests in the words of Gibbons' anthem:

> O Lord, increase my faith, strengthen me and confirm me in Thy true faith; endue me with wisdom, charity, and patience in all my adversity. Dear Jesus, say Amen.

A new wisdom, a new understanding with depth and breadth of vision, comes with God's mercy. New tendencies are felt, old perspectives are altered. And patience unfolds in ways which illuminate moments of joy, acts of love and bridges of relief which had been previously unnoticed.

The strength of Christian faith provides these new kinds of insights for countering the disruptions induced by our definitions of our rights and roles. We define ourselves along certain lines. Usually these definitions include a moral right to be treated with deference and comfort. We conceptualize our lives to be largely free from adversity, and our implicit understanding is that life will be good in accord with secular standards. Our whole vibrancy, geared to such definitions, is squelched as we find ourselves confronting broken expectations. Like broken promises, these disruptions can leave us distraught. Our roles lose their clarity, and we feel ourselves plunged into confusion.

New Outlooks and Goals

In consequence of all this, the Christian faith mediates the love of God to us in our brokenness by turning our attention to the "tools," the goals and the substance of our relations. Our attitudes shift through His grace. We look properly at those values by which we have been trying to order our lives. We look at the devices of desire by which we have been gauging our efforts to live a full life. We take stock of our purposes, and we likely discover how we have hardly suffered God to guide us.

It is this reordering of attitudes that brings insights. We perceive the mockery of our masks. In receiving God's love through the Christ in others we perceive new truths in our human relationships. God's power not only strengthens us in cheer but also enables us to lay aside certain pretensions. His presence is our joy; His love our comfort. In feeling His presence we neither need nor want to play games of fraud; we are His, and He knows us. With affirmation of this shift, the antidote of estrangement begins its effects.

We experience a second attitude of restoration in Christ, the *willingness to learn*. Human beings in their anguish may be led to reconditioning, to giving up old habits ingrained in them by their environments. This is a process of yielding their own wills to the will of God. Opening to God is the most helpful, most restorative therapeutic process in all that we portray as open-mindedness. Opening to God is the essence of wisdom, the route to patience, the channel of love. He is the Master Teacher through Christ, although we sometimes struggle in despair to block ourselves off from Him.

Learn to Love Again

We learn to feel love again as His love reaches across that dark, wide void spread before us, across that emptiness left after victories and joy have sped away from us. As creatures with enormous hurts, we are blind to the things which truly count, often even to our religious faith. But we know the *touch* of Jesus, as did the blind man on whom Jesus laid His hands twice. Why do we face troubles and deal with wrongs? We don't know. But we do know His tender touch. *And our response mirrors His response*—we feel love! "And he took the blind man by the hand and led him out of the village; and when he had spit on his eyes and laid his hands upon him, he asked him, 'Do you see anything'?" *(Mark 8;23).* Whatever may be the villages in which we are lost and blind, we may also need to be led away until He asks us, "Do you see anything?" Christ rekindles love and with it gives sight. This is the sight by which monstrous anxieties simply dissolve.

We have all known persons who appeared to be filled with tensions of resentment or malice or greed. The Christian person with magnified tensions will function almost as if he or she views surroundings only through cataracts. Anxiety sometimes clouds over the mind's eye to such a degree that we can no longer count our blessings, no longer feel a life of love. Some time ago a patient came loaded with dread and aching with fears, yet showing sound health physically. In his phychic misery this patient, a very successful man in his mid-forties, was turning his home and work into such a gloom that he was nearing suicide. His religious faith had become miniscule. He was asked if he would work as hard on his health spiritually with his spiritual leader in his congregation as he would work with me. In the months that followed, as he opened himself to God and deepened his faith, his sorting of other confusions produced the relief he had sought. "No more aches, no fears," he reported. "I know now who I am and what I am to be! Even my problems now are not heavy. Thank God for this victory."

We must overcome our hesitancy in looking at our conduct, our feelings and our bodily functions as connected to us in a whole way. The physical and psychological are diffused with the spiritual, and the wounds within one sector are influenced by conditions occurring in each of the others. It is pure ignorance to deny this interaction. More than one kind of treatment may be necessary before either relief or restoration can be brought. But when the complexity of a person's problems produces a severely despairing self, victory for the mending heart can be achieved through attention to both tissues and the spirit.

The Danger of Aberrations

We should pause to consider that rather massive blockages develop in psychological functioning when one in very intense urgency pursues religious learning excessively. The willingness to respond in Christian faith has been a stumbling block for certain personalities. These often prove to be individuals who represent a psychic history of great torment over many of their early years. The condition may be likened to that of a person who erupts (or attempts to erupt) in forty different directions at the same time. Whenever too much varied information is received indiscriminately, misunderstanding is likely to follow. Reaching out feverishly to absorb all kinds of teachings of a religious nature may yield great confusion.

A young married woman came to us after many years of medical and psychiatric treatment for depression. She had been converted to a deep Christian faith and reported receiving the Holy Spirit with the gift of speaking in tongues. She was extremely active in study groups and in reading religious literature almost every day of every week. Her marriage was suffering, and she was suffering from great anxieties and many irritabilities. She talked endlessly and confidently in judgmental terms. She expressed her fears at being hospitalized again. Her Christian fellowship practices took her periodically from one group to another. She claimed that she was open to God and that she wanted only to follow His will. In her words, Jesus Christ was not a stranger to her. There was such a frenzy to her faith that she appeared unable to receive composure enough to feel a wholeness in her faith. Certainly love was obscured and joy was elusive. In total health terms, she was miserable.

The first step in her recovery took place when she agreed to settle back into a program of moderation. Her attitudes were first examined carefully in the light of what she chose (after prayer and reflection) to be her main purposes as a child of God. In that process she directed her attention to her main obligations, aerating thoroughly the long-buried resentments that had been inflicting distorted images upon her as a wife and person. She was brought to a new understanding of her own temperament, distinguishing what came from her confusions and what came from God. With new, tested and selected definitions of her real self, she then went on to the second step—that of building a marriage in Christian fellowship and faith with her husband. As she relieved herself of excessive studying and often-contradictory teachings, her anxieties dissipated, her love renewed.

The Humbling Steps

I have known enough such tortured Christians so that I do not underestimate the difficulties in resolving such conflicts. Many of these people will validly claim an openness to God and a willingness to learn, yet their wretchedness continues. Still a third attitude of restoration in Christ is necessary, a blend of *surrender, asking and granting forgiveness and admission of loss of control.* Somehow, for many persons mending is withheld by their inability to take these humbling steps.

If I claim surrender intellectually, but do not yield emotionally to cry out for forgiveness, I may be holding on to an attitude which will continue to bar my healing. Then too, if I try to surrender without feeling and granting forgiveness to someone else who is involved in my conflicts, I will probably suffer on. And if I refuse to recognize my inability to exercise control along a certain line, I will be hindering my own recovery. The situation is this: until my attitudes include humbling myself before God, I will be less able to see the joy and love before me and my associates.

The dynamics of this fact are borne out in other patterns of human performance. As a cryptographer trainee, for example, I can hardly detect the hidden codes until you instruct me in their forms. I can hardly identify particular aircraft in flight until I have been trained in their distinctive features. I can hardly detect the malfunctions in a booming assembly line of manufacturing components unless I have first learned the patterns of sight and sound in those conditions. For a human being to become an open appreciater—one who appreciates the truth before him—he must first reach a sensitive state, a condition of readiness prerequisite to perceiving.

The human senses fail to produce sensible images that can be comprehended until the stage is inwardly set, until "the pump is primed." Alcoholic sufferers steadily refuse varied offers of help until they admit that they have lost control. Here is the surrender of self. A husband and a wife may grapple in conflict until they meet before God and each other to confess their respective sin and to ask forgiveness of each other and of God. Here we have rock-bottom surrender of self. Suffering, mourning or torment may precede the vision of honesty and truth so long avoided.

Understanding Clearly

One's life in misery tends to bring realization of real priorities. Bonhoeffer spoke of "genuine worship" as a goal emerging for him above all other prizes, a coming together of discipline through prayer, meditation and worship with compulsion equal to that of basic food and drink.[2] For Ernest Gordon this clarity of value came in stages from his fellow-prisoners. "For the first time I understood. . . . I was beginning to see that life is infinitely more complex, and at the same time more wonderful, than I had ever imagined. True, there was hatred. But there was also love. There was death, but there was also life. God had not left us. He was with us, calling us to live the divine life in fellowship. I was beginning to feel the miracle that God was working in the Death Camp by the River Kwai."[3] This insight came just after listening to a friend read to him from John's Letter: "There is no fear in love, but perfect love casts out fear. For fear has to do with punishment, and he who fears is not perfected in love. We love, because he first loved us. . . . And this commandment we have from him, that he who loves God should love his brother also" *(I John 4:18-21).*

From his experiences in prison in China for 2½ years, Langdon Gilkey singled out the effects of a person determining his deepest loyalty. This effect was one of discovering that the most important things in life are God's love and our neighbor's welfare. This comes to a solid significance by entrusting inner peace to the love of God alone. "A sense of significance that is rooted in the purposes of God cannot be lost in any situation."[4] This insight lifts up when a human being finally encounters Providence at work in particularly miserable situations.

The incredible perception of the late C.S. Lewis was never more evident than when he noted man's fatal modern habit of always looking *at* things, such as a beam of light, rather than also looking *along* them to the objects they illumine.[5] We often look at the light and what it illumines, but we seldom notice the *source* of the beam. In our misery and privation we need to behold the Source, the everpresent, only true Provider—God in His love. Under such conditions we cannot fail to observe how faint and short-lived are our many other previous sources of strength and joy.

Pleasure Versus Love and Joy

Around this planet swirl cultures of pleasure in which people become confused about the experience of joy and of love. We learn to pursue what we later find to be ephemeral privileges of pleasure. It is often hard to keep on having fun, for our fancies dry up, and then we look around for some new activity to soothe or stimulate our senses. We look for perquisites, those rarified rewards that signal our power and positions of esteem. These may be tax-free trips to a cabana in Spain, a company-leased limousine or perhaps simply the privilege of increasing power. The wholeness of a person disappears gradually in this kind of confusion, and the heart cannot mend.

Let us consider carefully what happens in the depths of our darkness. Pascal stated, "What shall we conclude from all our darkness, but our unworthiness?"[6] Where has our happiness gone? Christians find within the light of unworthiness the love of God. "Happiness is neither without us nor within us. It is in God, both without us and within us."[7] The soul has only rest with God. When we are most alone, most fragmented in despair, God is there. What an awesome, all-engulfing fact! What greater joy can there be for a human creature than this one? What can be more restorative? God's radiance never more clear fills His children with relief through love. Our darkness becomes a chamber of renewal.

God's love coming with wholeness marks a turning point, a reversal. In his analysis of conversion, Barclay describes the turning from darkness, idols and Satan to light and God as being a turning from frustration to victory.[8] Not only does man become conqueror of sin, he in this way becomes conqueror of the apparently unconquerable forces of misery. Barclay speaks of the report of Paul and Barnabas in their discussion of all that God had done *with* them in the realization of God as partner. It is this sense of God's championship that Christian sufferers feel and believe. "What a friend we have in Jesus" becomes a joyful experience.

Mending Through Love and Joy

The theme in this chapter is that love and joy facilitate mending. For those people who are distraught in desolation, the love of God's companionship is enlarged through suffering. The heart renews itself through pain. Suffering spawns compassion. In feeling God's compassionate presence, the sufferer finds abundant love, and in this love inestimable joy. It is this joy that brings the new strengths, the tenderness of healing.

Could you reflect back on your own past tribulations and not feel the seasoning, the heightened awareness by which you were brought to seeing new possibilities? While recalling momentarily the pathos of your ordeals, would you not also feel the growth and openness by which you were enabled to see beyond the ordinary? Just discovering the worth of self in the aftermath of unworthiness is that unique experience of being claimed by God. The whole history of Christianity resounds with this truth. With this love the mending heart becomes a weathered, enduring agent for extending love to others.

"Praise the Lord and hail His name in cheer!" *This* event is therapeutic. In the whole human spectrum can there be any greater process of joy than this event of knowing and loving God?

Martin Luther's lovely hymn requests:
> Make Thee a bed, soft undefiled,
> Within my heart that it may be
> A quiet chamber kept for Thee.

Here is the attitude gained by those Christians who turn to God. Here is the form of loving God by letting Him love us. God in the heart is the only Healer, the only joy from which all substantial joy arises.

The Shape of Love

The shape of love for those who turn to look for it is still cast against the sky on Calvary. Those who would minister to the wounded or despondent today, whatever their special gifts, may still trace the love expanding out of suffering by God's Son. Love's configuration is service, unto death if necessary, and always above self. Where else, how else, why else do we find love?

The God of Christian worship provides forgiving, unearned love. When we are tended, we are being mended. His mercy is restorative. When we tend to someone else, then we are also being mended. When a human being knows the love of

Christ, in either being tended or tending, he is restored, to be filled with "all the fullness of God" (*Ephesians 3:19*).

The story is told of the young soldier who lay dying in the freezing blizzard winds on a forsaken stretch of Russian soil during the torturous retreat of the French troops under Bonaparte. One comrade from a passing string of demoralized infantry troops stepped aside into the gloom, sat beside the young lad and covered his shivering body with the short remnant of his own tunic. "Are you cold now?" he asked. "Not with you here," came the grateful reply. God's comfort does reach down to the sufferers, even when they remain in cold, hunger or pain, just as His love follows us into our predicaments. Is there any warmer joy than that of serving a fellow creature in his hurt? Is there any truer joy than that kindled by the fire of love?

Love in Action

The curative powers of love have long been hailed by authorities. The deficiency of the "vitamin of love" is responsible for mental disorders. And in much of mental therapy love is regarded as that vital element in the effects of empathy, sympathy, kindness and mutual trust as these feelings contribute to more harmonious relations.[9] Those broken in heart, spirit and hope—the intensely angry, highly confused and despairing—these may not know one spark of joy until they feel the creative warmth of love in their spirit. It may require a word, someone's hand or smile, or their own prayer and thought. But mending can commence when this creation, this dawn of contact with God, takes place in their hearts. This commencement comes with the *realization that God is present with those who suffer*; He is there sharing and bearing.

Noted author, minister and retreat leader, Lee Whiston put the point with gentle clarity in these words: "It is no longer God looking at us from His point of view, but God in Jesus coming down in human flesh so that God could love humanity from our point of view."[10] The genius of the Incarnation, Whiston offers, lies in this shift of position, one that enables human beings to feel loved from within. The presence of the Holy Spirit within us brings that special comfort of being cared for by someone near at hand.

Realization of this shift of position means identifying with God in His promises and in His strength.

But to fail to realize this shift is to deny the joy of faith for the struggle.

The Test of Faith

Through our pains and struggles our faith is put to the test. In James Agee's novel *A Death in The Family*, Mary is being comforted by her family after learning that her husband has been killed instantly in a car wreck.[11] Suddenly Mary cries out, "Oh, God, *forgive* me. . . . It's just more than I can bear!" Her Aunt Hannah draws close to console her, saying that Mary has nothing to ask forgiveness for, that God would never ask her not to grieve.

Mary replies that she had spoken to God as if He had no mercy, "As if He were trying to rub it in, to torment me. That's what I asked forgiveness for."

Her aunt bends low to whisper, "Our Lord on the Cross, do you remember?"

"My God, my God, why hast Thou forsaken me?"

"Yes.... What was it He said...? The very next thing He said."

"Father, into Thy hand I commend my spirit," Mary said, taking her hands from her face and looking meekly at her aunt. Right here is the *joy* of faith, the spark of healing comfort.

This incident illustrates how pain can lead to rebuke or to turning from God. Yet often someone else comes to help us confront ourselves, to answer the test of our faith.

In his very moving play *J.B.*, Archibald MacLeish draws attention to this spark that lies within the heart. Sarah says:

> Blow on the coal of the heart.
> The candles in churches are out.
> The lights have gone out in the sky.
> Blow on the coal of the heart
> And we'll see by and by....

J.B. then adds:

> We'll see where we are.
> The wit won't burn and the wet soul smoulders.
> Blow on the coal of the harth and we'll know ...
> We'll know....[12]

When our knowledge and our humor have been rendered inert, and when the tears of anguish prevail, our vision is restored as we see again by this spark of love remaining in the mending heart.

Sight cannot be denied when this spark is fanned with the affirming joy of faith. The *joy of belief* becomes the renewal of understanding. It is born out of hardship, and man can have no authentic understanding without it.

The Joy of The Lord

The beautiful oyster-catcher, a shore bird that feeds on mussel shells, depends for survival on its long, sharp thin bill to penetrate the crevice opening of a mussel to cut the abductor and lift out the helpless flesh. Whether oyster-catchers are hammerers (who hammer into the crevice) or stabbers (who pierce as if by stabbing the shell), they show the individualized method of their parents, and *all* require this instinctive response to survive. So too in human beings: there is an instinctive assistance to healing in reuniting with God's love. Some would know this spark to be *hope*, but it is a catalyst for all other mending efforts. We may go about our probing in the darkness in vastly different ways. But the glow of returning to God with His endless love is never brighter than when we probe in our darkness and find Him once more.

Christianity is not a mere dream, nor is it a surrender to a materialistic reality. It is instead a concrete experience centered in and through the heart. The mending of hearts thus takes the Christian to the Master of the heart through surrender to God, devotion, suffering, service and joy. The gift of Jesus Christ is the most powerful gift in all of human history.

Whatever other loss of loved ones, or of limbs, or

of victories or of freedom there may be, the despairing self is restored through God's power. "When I sit in darkness, the Lord will be a light to me. I will bear the indignation of the Lord because I have sinned against him, until he pleads my cause and executes judgment for me. He will bring me forth to the light; I shall behold his deliverance" *(Micah 7:8,9.)* Awareness of personal quality of being and of personal belonging lifts the Christian from all pain, "for to live is Christ." It is the story of love triumphing out of love.

Fulfillment in Christ

We return again and again to the importance of the ideas by which we live and to which we assign priority. Religious conversion leads to fulfillment in Christ, to a bridge that spans all adversity. The ideas of Christ can and do mend us in our brokenness as we lovingly cherish His presence.

The unconditional love of God for us, as an awareness in our hearts, is the countermending force by which we are mended. It gives us peace. Through it we are able to see once more, as if it were a frame surrounding our outlook and always influencing all that we see. C.S. Lewis once noted that the whole point in *seeing through something* is to *see something through it*, but he failed to allow for the powerful effect of framing. What a person experiences visually is dramatically altered by the framing through which he sees it. God's unconditional love for us through Christ effects a reconciling health in everything that we experience. The hostility and antagonisms beneath our broken hearts give way to His peace. When Christ becomes the frame or window by which we view all of life, our joy is His blessedness.

Many times we need to ponder, as did A.M. Hunter, whether Christian goodness differs from non-Christian goodness. The human forces of health, hope, love, courage and joy do succumb to the conditions of life. Theology may get haywire, and mine may not avoid certain contradictory assertions, but the hazards of despair cannot withstand the very special spiritual force of God working through Jesus Christ. Hunter likens the law of Christ—to bear one another's burdens—to the fulfillment one derives from using a compass.[13]

In the depths of despair, human beings yearn for a compass to provide both direction and hope. The Christian's compass, perhaps unlike that used by others in misery, brings a healing conviction. In coming to Christ and His compass, one comes to peace with life. All human creatures who cherish justice, kindness and human rights may call upon God's mercy expectantly—and receive it. But for those who choose to walk humbly with God through Christ, the divine Compass will guide and restore the soul with greater living proof than any other known to mankind. May it be so for you.

---

1. George Santayana, *Soliloquies in England and Later Soliloquies* (New York: Scribner's, 1922), pp. 133-34.
2. Dietrich Bonhoeffer, *Letters and Papers from Prison*, 3rd ed. (New York: Macmillan, 1967), p. 181.
3. Gordon, *Through the Valley of the Kwai*, p. 113.
5. Walter Hooper, ed., *C.S. Lewis: The Dark Tower and Other Stories* (New York: Harcourt Brace Jovanovich, 1977), p. 10.
6. *Pensees*, No. 557.
7. *Pensees*, No. 465.

8. Barclay, *Turning to God*, p. 31.
9. Piritrim Sorokin, "The Powers of Creative Unselfish Love," in A. Maslow, ed., *New Knowledge in Human Values* (New York: Harper & Bros., 1959), p. 8.
10. Lee Whiston, "Shifting Our Position," in *Faith at Work*, Oct. 1977, pp. 24-25.
11. James Agee, *A Death in the Family* (New York: Avon, 1938), p. 128.
12. Archibald MacLeish, *J.B.* (Boston: Houghton Mifflin, 1956), p. 153.
13. A.M. Hunter, *Gleanings from the New Testament* (Philadelphia: Westminster, 1975), pp. 175-76.

Notes

OTHER GOOD BOOKS
FROM HARVEST HOUSE

☐ **BE THE WOMAN YOU WANT TO BE,** Ruthe White. Some women set out to resolve all their problems on their knees, in scroungy bathrobes and unkempt hair. Others seek to win their victories in the beauty shop, at the lingerie counter or in a spa. Somewhere inbetween is a balance. This book presents that balanced perspective that helps you exercise your individual right to a rediscovery of yourself. 1148—$2.95 (paper)

☐ **THEY SAW THE SECOND COMING,** Doug Clark. A remarkable candid description of the unfolding of events leading up to the final moments of earth's civilizations! The step-by-step build-up of the world's most powerful dictator—the Antichrist—and his cold-blooded grasp for world domination, then simply for survival. The most magnificent description ever put in print of the second coming of the Messiah! 1903—$3.95 (paper)

☐ **HOW TO ENRICH YOUR MARRIAGE,** Margaret Hardisty. The author of the bestseller, **Forever My Love,** is joined by her attorney-husband as they answer some of the hundreds of questions they have encountered in conducting seminars across the country. This book encourages an enriched marriage through proper use of one's channels of communication. 1385—$2.95 (paper)

☐ **THE ART OF MARRIED LOVE,** Pamela Heim. Only two perfect people can experience a perfect marriage. The rest of us have to work at it. This book is for those willing to get moving and press toward the objective—oneness. When God is present, His love is present. And God's presence will enhance, purify and beautify the natural love of any couple. 1520—$2.95 (paper)

☐ **LETTERS ON LIFE AND LOVE,** Dr. James Kilgore. A Christian psychologist shares personal letters from women that have been received and answered by him regarding the problem areas of life and love. Dr. Kilgore deals honestly and openly with some of the very touchy personal questions that women want to know about, but are often afraid to ask. This small book should be very helpful to thousands of women. 1121—$1.75 (mass)

☐ **GETTING TO KNOW YOU, A Guide to Communicating.** Meaningful relationships established on a healthy one-to-one basis through the neglected ways of communication is the central theme of this unique book by Dr. Marjorie Umphrey. Helps are offered on breaking down barriers of communication—with you spouse, your peers and your children. 0257—$2.95 (paper)

Harvest House Publishers
2861 McGaw
Irvine, Ca. 92714